S. Hrg. 114–78

GETTING IT RIGHT ON DATA SECURITY AND BREACH NOTIFICATION LEGISLATION IN THE 114TH CONGRESS

HEARING

BEFORE THE

SUBCOMMITTEE ON CONSUMER PROTECTION, PRODUCT SAFETY, INSURANCE, AND DATA SECURITY

OF THE

COMMITTEE ON COMMERCE, SCIENCE, AND TRANSPORTATION UNITED STATES SENATE

ONE HUNDRED FOURTEENTH CONGRESS

FIRST SESSION

FEBRUARY 5, 2015

Printed for the use of the Committee on Commerce, Science, and Transportation

U.S. GOVERNMENT PUBLISHING OFFICE

96–892 PDF   WASHINGTON : 2015

For sale by the Superintendent of Documents, U.S. Government Publishing Office
Internet: bookstore.gpo.gov   Phone: toll free (866) 512–1800; DC area (202) 512–1800
Fax: (202) 512–2104   Mail: Stop IDCC, Washington, DC 20402–0001

SENATE COMMITTEE ON COMMERCE, SCIENCE, AND TRANSPORTATION

ONE HUNDRED FOURTEENTH CONGRESS

FIRST SESSION

JOHN THUNE, South Dakota, *Chairman*

ROGER F. WICKER, Mississippi	BILL NELSON, Florida, *Ranking*
ROY BLUNT, Missouri	MARIA CANTWELL, Washington
MARCO RUBIO, Florida	CLAIRE McCASKILL, Missouri
KELLY AYOTTE, New Hampshire	AMY KLOBUCHAR, Minnesota
TED CRUZ, Texas	RICHARD BLUMENTHAL, Connecticut
DEB FISCHER, Nebraska	BRIAN SCHATZ, Hawaii
JERRY MORAN, Kansas	EDWARD MARKEY, Massachusetts
DAN SULLIVAN, Alaska	CORY BOOKER, New Jersey
RON JOHNSON, Wisconsin	TOM UDALL, New Mexico
DEAN HELLER, Nevada	JOE MANCHIN, West Virginia
CORY GARDNER, Colorado	GARY PETERS, Michigan
STEVE DAINES, Montana	

DAVID SCHWIETERT, *Republican Staff Director*
NICK ROSSI, *Republican Deputy Staff Director*
REBECCA SEIDEL, *Republican General Counsel*
JASON VAN BEEK, *Republican Deputy General Counsel*
KIM LIPSKY, *Democratic Staff Director*
CHRIS DAY, *Democratic Deputy Staff Director*
CLINT ODOM, *Democratic General Counsel and Policy Director*

————

SUBCOMMITTEE ON CONSUMER PROTECTION, PRODUCT SAFETY, INSURANCE, AND DATA SECURITY [1]

JERRY MORAN, Kansas, *Chairman*	RICHARD BLUMENTHAL, Connecticut, *Ranking*
ROY BLUNT, Missouri	
TED CRUZ, Texas	CLAIRE McCASKILL, Missouri
DEB FISCHER, Nebraska	AMY KLOBUCHAR, Minnesota
DEAN HELLER, Nevada	EDWARD MARKEY, Massachusetts
DAN SULLIVAN, Alaska	CORY BOOKER, New Jersey
CORY GARDNER, Colorado	TOM UDALL, New Mexico
STEVE DAINES, Montana	

[1] On March 3, 2015 the Committee finalized Member assignments for its subcommittees. The list below reflects March 3, 2015 assignments. When this hearing was held, on February 5, 2015, formal assignments had not yet been made.

CONTENTS

GETTING IT RIGHT ON DATA SECURITY AND BREACH NOTIFICATION LEGISLATION IN THE 114TH CONGRESS

THURSDAY, FEBRUARY 5, 2015

U.S. SENATE,
SUBCOMMITTEE ON CONSUMER PROTECTION, PRODUCT
SAFETY, INSURANCE, AND DATA SECURITY,
COMMITTEE ON COMMERCE, SCIENCE, AND TRANSPORTATION,
Washington, DC.

The Subcommittee met, pursuant to notice, at 10 a.m. in room SR–253, Russell Senate Office Building, Hon. Jerry Moran, presiding.

Present: Senators Moran [presiding], Thune, Blunt, Fischer, Daines, Klobuchar, Blumenthal, and Schatz.

OPENING STATEMENT OF HON. JERRY MORAN, U.S. SENATOR FROM KANSAS

Senator MORAN. As I indicated, this is the first subcommittee hearing I have chaired in 8 years in Congress, and I was nervous, apparently nervous enough not to turn on the microphone.

We look forward to being educated and getting a good understanding. First, I want to thank my colleagues and their level of interest in this important topic. I would also like to thank, as I said, our witnesses for joining us today. Expertise is important to us as Members of Congress, and unfortunately, this is a very timely topic.

The purpose of this hearing is in many ways somewhat narrow, it is to examine the merits of the Federal data security standard and the need for preemptive and uniform Federal data breach notification.

We all know we live in a digital world where consumers have embraced online products and services. Kansans, my folks at home, they know they can make purchases, determine their credit score, conduct banking and examine health care plans all from a mobile phone, computer, or a tablet. That is true of consumers across the country and increasingly around the globe.

This digital economy creates new risks. In a world where one bad actor can battle against a team of highly trained experts, we face challenges to make certain that consumers are protected and that businesses have the tools and incentives to protect their customers from harm.

(1)

For more than a decade, Congress, the Commerce Committee in particular, has been contemplating issues surrounding data security and data breach notification.

In 2004, the Committee held its first congressional hearing to examine the high profile breach of ChoicePoint, a data aggregation firm. This breach forced the first of many conversations here in Congress, and today, we continue that dialogue.

Recent high profile data breaches as well as the headline grabbing Sony cyberattack from late last year are the latest examples that highlight the ongoing and serious cyber threats that face Americans and businesses.

Just this morning, we woke up to news of what experts are calling the largest health care breach to date. This time, the cyber criminals were able to infiltrate the nation's second largest health insurer to steal names, birth dates, medical I.D.'s, Social Security numbers, street addresses, e-mail addresses, and employment information, including income data.

These high profile breaches are the most severe of what have become a common occurrence in our digital society. As of 2015, the Privacy Rights Clearinghouse has estimated more than 4,400 breaches involving more than 932 million records that have been made public since 2005.

The Verizon 2014 data breach investigation report reviewed more than 63,000 security incidents and found 1,367 confirmed data breaches in 2013. On average, that is just shy of four breaches every day.

While Congress has developed sector specific data security requirements for both financial institutions and companies that handle particular types of health information, Congress has been unable to reach consensus on the development of national data security and data breach notification standards.

As a result, states have taken on this task by developing their own standards and as of today, businesses are subjected to a patchwork of over 50 different state, district, and territory laws that determine how businesses must notify consumers in the event of a breach. In addition, 12 states have enacted laws regarding data security practices.

The need for Federal action becomes clearer each day. Last month President Obama voiced his support for national data breach notification legislation with strong preemptive language in part because he recognizes the benefits to American consumers and businesses of a predictable uniform data breach notice.

The President's support along with bipartisan and bicameral congressional interest has renewed optimism among stakeholders that Congress can develop a balanced and thoughtful approach with legislation in the near term.

Today, we will focus our attention on some of the key questions and topics of this debate, including what are the benefits of a national data breach notification standard? Should Congress implement a basic data security standard, to whom should that standard apply, should the Federal standard preempt state standards?

What should be the trigger for notification, specific conditions that represent a potential harm to consumers, should there be exemptions and safe harbors, if so, for who, in what circumstances?

Within what time-frame should a company be required to notify consumers?

Should Congress enact new or stronger penalties for enforcement authorities and remedies? What lessons can we learn from states that have implemented their own data breach notification standards?

I am confident that our panel with its expertise can share valuable insight into those questions and others that the Committee members may have, and help us find the right balance to these issues.

I would like to recognize the Subcommittee's Ranking Member, Senator Blumenthal, for him to deliver his opening statement, and I would indicate to Senator Blumenthal here in public as we have in private, that I look forward to working very closely with you in a very thoughtful and bipartisan way to see that our Subcommittee accomplishes good things for the country.

STATEMENT OF HON. RICHARD BLUMENTHAL, U.S. SENATOR FROM CONNECTICUT

Senator BLUMENTHAL. Thank you. First of all, my thanks to Senator Moran for his leadership, and in a very bipartisan way, for reaching out to me and also convening this subcommittee on a critically important topic. I really look forward to his continued insight and very thoughtful leadership on consumer protection issues. I am proud to serve as the Ranking Member of this very important subcommittee.

I have served on this subcommittee for two years now. It is critical to consumer issues that affect every day Americans. We have delved into the General Motors' recall and the deadly Takata airbags.

Today, the issue of data breach is no less central to American lives, even if it seems somewhat less spectacular. 2014 was known as the year of the data breach. The importance of this issue was brought home, as Senator Moran said, just this morning when we read about the Anthem breach, which is absolutely breathtaking in its scope and scale.

It is not only breathtaking but mind-bending in its extent and potential impact, and it is potentially heartbreaking for consumers who may be affected, not only birthdays, addresses, e-mail and employment information, but also Social Security numbers and income data were taken from Anthem, and potentially, although the company has said there is no evidence of it so far, critical health information.

This breach comes after J.P. Morgan indicated a loss of personal information to hackers of about 83 million households.

Of course, in November, hackers, the United States Government has said, had ties to the North Korean government, orchestrated a disruptive attack on Sony. The Sony attack would be comedy, but it is literally no laughing matter to other businesses, including financial institutions on Wall Street, health insurers and others whose vital data may be taken.

To quote the FBI Agent in New York, Leo Taddeo, who supervises the Cyber and Special Operations Division, "We are losing ground in the battle with hackers."

In December 2013, we first learned about Target's data breach, which affected credit card information and personal contact information for as many as 110 million consumers.

The point here is that these losses of data are not only losses to these companies; they are potentially life changing losses to consumers. Target, J.P. Morgan, and Anthem failed not only the companies, but they failed their customers and consumers when these data breaches occurred.

This fact of life is more than the cost of doing business for these companies. It is an invasion of their privacy. It is an invasion of consumer privacy, potentially theft of identity and personal assets.

The billions of dollars that could have been saved by consumers, creditors, banks, and others if companies and universities who were collecting sensitive data spent money and resources on better protecting that information is one of the facts that brings us here today.

As Attorney General, I brought a number of enforcement cases against companies that violated Connecticut's data breach law. I worked with my colleagues, including Lisa Madigan, who is here today, and I express special appreciation to her for her great work in this area, and I worked with Kelly Ayotte, who is now a colleague.

This issue is hardly a partisan one. In fact, it is distinctly bipartisan, involving stronger protections for sensitive consumer data, and we recognize the states as laboratories of democracy and the great work they have done in this area.

Let me just conclude by saying I think we have a lot of work that needs to be done, a lot of good work that should be done, but one guiding principle is: first do no harm. That is do no harm to the state protections and state enforcers who every day are seeking to protect their citizens from the scourge and spreading problem of data theft, in order for consumers to trust retailers, banks, and online sales, they need to know their data is secure without abuse, whether they are shopping online or at a bricks and mortar stores.

Consumers expect retailers collecting their sensitive personal information will do everything in their power to protect that data. That is a reasonable expectation. They have a right to expect better than they are now receiving from retailers, companies, insurers, banks, all of the institutions, including universities and non-profits that increasingly have the coin of the realm, which is data about consumers.

Thank you, Mr. Chairman.

Senator MORAN. Thank you, Senator Blumenthal. We now will turn to our witnesses. With us today is Ms. Cheri F. McGuire. She is Vice President of Global Government Affairs and Cybersecurity Policy for Symantec Corporation.

Mr. Mallory Duncan, Senior Vice President and General Counsel of the National Retail Federation.

Dr. Ravi Pendse, who is the Chief Information Officer at Brown University, but easier for me to say Wichita State University, his previous employer.

Ms. Yael Weinman, Vice President for Global Privacy and General Counsel, Information Technology Industry Council.

The Honorable Lisa Madigan, the Attorney General of the State of Illinois, and finally, Mr. Doug Johnson, Senior Vice President and Senior Advisor for Risk Management Policy, Office of the Chief Economist of the American Bankers Association.

Ms. McGuire, let's begin with you.

STATEMENT OF CHERI F. McGUIRE, VICE PRESIDENT, GLOBAL GOVERNMENT AFFAIRS AND CYBERSECURITY POLICY, SYMANTEC CORPORATION

Ms. McGuire. Thank you so much, Chairman Moran, Ranking Member Blumenthal, and members of the Subcommittee. Thank you for the opportunity to testify today on this very important issue.

As the largest security software company in the world, Symantec's global intelligence network is made up of millions of sensors that give us an unique view of the entire Internet threat landscape.

As we all have seen, even as of this morning, the recent headlines about cyber attacks have focused mostly on data breaches across a spectrum of industries. These network intrusions that result in stolen data have deep and profound impacts for the individuals who must worry about and clean up their identities, for the organizations whose systems have been penetrated, and for the governments trying to establish the right notification policies as well as deter and apprehend the perpetrators.

The magnitude of threats of personally identifiable information is unprecedented. Over just the past 2 years alone, the number of identities exposed through network breaches is approaching one billion. Those are just the ones we know about.

While many assume breaches are the result of sophisticated malware or well-resourced state actor, the reality is much more troubling. According to a recent report from the Online Trust Alliance, 90 percent of last year's breaches could have been prevented if organizations implemented basic cybersecurity best practices.

While the focus on data breaches and the identities put at risk is certainly warranted, we also must not lose sight of the other types of cyber attacks that are equally concerning and can have dangerous consequences.

There are a wide set of tools available to the cyber attacker, and the incidents we see today range from basic confidence schemes to massive denial of service attacks to sophisticated and potentially destructive intrusions into critical infrastructure systems.

The attackers, of course, run the gamut and include highly organized criminal enterprises, disgruntled employees, individual cyber criminals, so-called "hacktivists," and state-sponsored groups.

While the continuing onslaught of data breaches is well documented, what seems to get less attention are the causes of data breaches and what can be done to prevent them. Targeted attacks are the single largest cause, most of which rely on social engineering, or in simple terms, tricking people into doing something they would not do if fully aware of the consequences of their actions.

Last year, nearly 60 percent of data breaches occurred through network intrusions by unauthorized users. Another major cause is a lack of basic computer hygiene practices. While good security will stop most of these attacks, which often seek to exploit older known vulnerabilities, many organizations do not have up-to-date security or patch systems, do not make full use of the security tools available to them, or have security unevenly applied throughout their enterprise.

What can we do? Cybersecurity is about managing risk, assessing one's risk and developing a plan is essential. For organizations, there are many guidelines including, as you discussed yesterday, the NIST Cybersecurity Framework, the FCC guidelines for small businesses, the Online Trust Alliance data protection and breach readiness guide, and many others.

For the individual, we provide resources for managing online security to our Norton customers, and the FTC and others have many tips available on their websites. In fact, just this week the SEC published best practices for individual investors to secure their online accounts. In short, there is no shortage of available resources.

Strong security should include intrusion protection, reputation based security, behavioral based blocking, data encryption backups, and data loss prevention tools. While the criminals' tactics are constantly evolving, basic cyber hygiene is still the simplest and most cost effective first step.

Turning to the policy landscape, Symantec supports, as you said, Chairman Moran, a balanced and thoughtful national standard for data breach notification built on three principles.

First, the scope of any legislation should apply equally to all entities that collect, maintain, or sell significant numbers of records containing sensitive personal information. This covers both the Government and private sector.

Second, implementing pre-breach security measures should be central to any legislation. New legislation should not simply require notifications of consumers in case of a breach, but should seek to minimize the likelihood of a breach in the first place.

Third, encryption or other proven security measures that render data unreadable and unusable at rest or in transit should be a key element to establish the risk based threshold for notification. This limits the burden for both consumers and for the breached organizations.

At Symantec, we are committed to improving online security across the globe, and we will continue to work collaboratively with our partners on ways to do so.

Thank you again for the opportunity to testify today, and I will look forward to your questions later.

[The prepared statement of Ms. McGuire follows:]

PREPARED STATEMENT OF CHERI F. MCGUIRE, VICE PRESIDENT, GLOBAL GOVERNMENT AFFAIRS AND CYBERSECURITY POLICY, SYMANTEC CORPORATION

Chairman Moran, Ranking Member Blumenthal, distinguished members of the Committee, thank you for the opportunity to testify today on behalf of Symantec Corporation.

My name is Cheri McGuire and I am the Vice President for Global Government Affairs and Cybersecurity Policy at Symantec. I am responsible for Symantec's global public policy agenda and government engagement strategy, which includes cybersecurity, data integrity, critical infrastructure protection (CIP), and privacy. I lead a team of professionals spanning the U.S., Canada, Europe, and Asia, and represent the company in key policy organizations. In this capacity, I work extensively with industry and government organizations, and currently serve on the World Economic Forum Global Agenda Council on Cybersecurity, as well as on the boards of the Information Technology Industry Council, the U.S. Information Technology Office (USITO) in China, and the National Cyber Security Alliance. From 2010 to 2012, I was Chair of the Information Technology Sector Coordinating Council—one of 16 critical sectors identified by the President and the U.S. Department of Homeland Security (DHS) to partner with the government on CIP and cybersecurity. I am also a past board member of the IT Information Sharing and Analysis Center (IT–ISAC). Previously, I served in various positions at DHS, including as head of the National Cyber Security Division and U.S. Computer Emergency Readiness Team (US–CERT).

Symantec protects much of the world's information, and is a global leader in security, backup and availability solutions. We are the largest security software company in the world, with over 32 years of experience developing Internet security technology and helping consumers, businesses and governments secure and manage their information and identities. Our products and services protect people's information and their privacy across platforms—from the smallest mobile device, to the enterprise data center, to cloud-based systems. We have established some of the most comprehensive sources of Internet threat data in the world through our Global Intelligence Network, which is comprised of millions of attack sensors recording thousands of events per second, and we maintain 10 Security Response Centers around the globe. In addition, we process billions of e-mail messages and web requests across our 14 global data centers. All of these resources allow us to capture worldwide security data that give our analysts a unique view of the entire Internet threat landscape.

The hearing today not only is timely—given the recent high profile data breaches—but also is a critically important discussion that will help focus attention on what businesses can do to protect themselves from similar attacks and how Congress can craft effective data breach legislation. Symantec welcomes the opportunity to provide comments to the Committee as it looks at how to prevent and respond to data breaches.

In my testimony today, I will discuss:

- The current cyber threat landscape;
- How breaches are happening, including the methods criminals are using to steal data;
- Security measures to protect data and prevent breaches; and
- Key elements for data breach legislation.

The Current Cyber Threat Landscape

Most of the recent headlines about cyber attacks have focused on data breaches across the spectrum of industries, which have become an all too common occurrence. Breaches impact individuals whose identities have been stolen, the organizations with systems that have been penetrated, and governments that are seeking ways to set data breach policies and to apprehend the perpetrators. Organizations that suffered significant breaches over the past few years include the State of South Carolina, Target, Neiman Marcus, Michael's, Home Depot, and Sony, just to name a few.

The theft of personally identifiable information (PII) over this time-frame is simply unprecedented—over just the past two years alone, the number of identities exposed through breaches will likely approach *one billion.* And this is just from known breaches as many go unreported or undetected. Recent data breaches have touched all parts of society and across the globe, from governments and businesses to celebrities and individual's households. While many assume that breaches are the result of sophisticated malware or a well-resourced state actor, the reality is much more troubling. According to a recent report from the Online Trust Alliance, 90 percent of last year's breaches could have been prevented if organizations implemented basic cybersecurity best practices.[1]

In addition, the statistics from our 2014 Internet Security Threat Report are clear that the cyber threats we are facing on a day to day basis are growing. More than 550 million identities were exposed in 2013, which was an increase of 62 percent over the prior year, and the top eight breaches exposed more than 10 million identities each. These breaches often exposed real names, birth dates and/or government ID numbers (*e.g.,* social security numbers). Some records also exposed other highly sensitive data, such as medical records or financial information.

---

[1] *https://www.otalliance.org/news-events/press-releases/ota-determines-over-90-data-breaches-2014-could-have-been-prevented*

While the focus on data breaches and the identities put at risk is certainly warranted, we also must not lose sight of the other types of cyber attacks that are equally concerning and can have dangerous consequences. There are a wide set of tools available to the cyber attacker, and the incidents we see today range from basic confidence schemes to massive denial of service attacks to sophisticated (and potentially destructive) intrusions into critical infrastructure systems. The economic impact can be immediate with the theft of money, or more long term and structural, such as through the theft of intellectual property. It can ruin a company or individual's reputation or finances, and it can impact citizens' trust in the Internet and their government.

The attackers run the gamut and include highly organized criminal enterprises, disgruntled employees, individual cybercriminals, so-called "hacktivists," and state-sponsored groups. The motivations vary—the criminals generally are looking for some type of financial gain, the hacktivists are seeking to promote or advance some cause, and the state actors can be engaged in espionage (traditional spycraft or economic) or infiltrating critical infrastructure systems. These lines, however, are not set in stone, as criminals and even state actors might pose as hacktivists, and criminals often offer their skills to the highest bidder. Attribution has always been difficult in cyberspace, and is further complicated by the ability of cyber actors to mask their motives and objectives through misdirection and obfuscation.

How Data Breaches are Occurring

While the continuing onslaught of data breaches is well documented, what is less understood is why data breaches happen and what can be done to prevent them. Targeted attacks remain a major cause. Some are direct attacks on a company's servers, where attackers search for unpatched vulnerabilities on websites or undefended connections to the Internet. But most rely on social engineering—in the simplest of terms, tricking people into doing something they would not do if fully aware of the consequences of their actions. E-mail is still a major attack vector and can take the form of broad mailings ("phishing") or highly targeted messages ("spear phishing"). More and more we see the latter variety, with publicly available information used to craft an e-mail designed to dupe a specific victim or group of victims. The goal of both varieties is to get victims to open an infected file or go to a malicious or compromised website.

Another major cause of breaches is a lack of basic computer hygiene practices. While good security will stop most of these attacks—which often seek to exploit older, known vulnerabilities—many organizations do not have up-to-date security or patched systems, do not make full use of the security tools available to them, or have security unevenly applied throughout their enterprise. Even today—despite the recent focus on the loss of personal information—a large segment of the workforce handles sensitive information on unprotected mobile devices, servers, desktops, and laptops.

E-mail, web mail, and removable storage devices are another source of breaches. Most of us, at one time or another, have e-mailed something to our personal e-mail address from our office so that we can work on it later. If our e-mail accounts or home computers are compromised, or if we misplace the thumb drive we use to transport files, any sensitive, unencrypted data is now lost and our organization suffers a data breach. And of course, breaches can occur through outright theft, often by a fired or disgruntled employee.

Cybercriminals are also targeting the places where we "live and play" online in order to get at sensitive personal data. Social media is an increasingly sinister tool for cybercriminals. It is particularly effective in direct attacks, as people tend to trust things that appear to come from a friend's social media feed. But social media is also widely used to conduct reconnaissance for spear phishing or other targeted attacks. It can provide just the kind of personal details that a skilled attacker can use to get a victim to let his or her guard down. The old cliché is true when it comes to cyber attacks: we have to be right 100 percent of the time in protecting ourselves, while the attacker only has to get it right once.

Security Measures to Protect Data and Prevent Breaches

Cybersecurity is about managing risk, whether at the individual or the organizational level. Assessing one's risk and developing a plan is essential. For the individual, the Federal Trade Commission's website is an excellent starting point for doing so.[2] The website provides educational resources for how to better protect your

---

[2] *http://www.consumer.ftc.gov/topics/privacy-identity*

identity and privacy online as well as helpful tools to help you report and recover if your personal information is ever stolen.

For organizations of any size, the NIST Cyber Security Framework[3], developed by industry and government in 2014 and in which Symantec was an active contributor, provides a solid structure for risk management. It lays out five core cybersecurity functions (Identify, Protect, Detect, Respond and Recover) that all organizations can use to plan for managing cyber events and protecting against data breaches, as well as useful references to international standards. As detailed below, good security starts with the basics and includes measures specific to one's needs.

Basic Security Steps

When it comes to security, it starts with the basics. Though criminals' tactics are continually evolving, good cyber hygiene is still the simplest and most cost-effective first step. Strong passwords remain the foundation of good security—on home and work devices, e-mail, social media accounts, or whatever you use to communicate (or really anything you log into). And these passwords must be different, because using a single password means that a breach of one account exposes all of your accounts. Using a second authentication factor (whether through a text message, a smart card, biometrics, or a token with a changing numeric password) significantly increases the security of a login.

Patch management is also vital. Individuals and organizations should not delay installing patches, or software updates, because the same patch that closes a vulnerability can be a roadmap for a criminal to exploit and compromise any unpatched devices. The reality is that a large percentage of computers around the world, including some in large organizations, do not get patched regularly, and cybercriminals count on this. While so-called "zero day exploits"—previously unknown critical vulnerabilities—get the most press, it is older, unpatched vulnerabilities that cause most systems to get compromised.

Modern Security Software

Poor or insufficiently deployed security can also lead to a breach, and a modern security suite that is being fully utilized is also essential. While most people still commonly refer to security software as "anti-virus" or AV, advanced security protection is much more than that. In the past, the same piece of malware would be delivered to thousands or even millions of computers. Today, cybercriminals can take the same malware and create unlimited unique variants that can slip past basic AV software. If all your security software does is check for signatures (or digital fingerprints) of known malware, you are by definition not protected against even moderately sophisticated attacks. Put differently, a check-the-box security program that only includes installation of basic AV software may give you piece of mind—but that is about all it will give you.

Modern security software does much more than look for known malware: it monitors your system, watching for unusual Internet traffic, activity, or system processes that could be indicative of malicious activity. At Symantec we also use what we call *Insight* and *SONAR,* which are reputation-based and behavior-based heuristic security technologies. Insight is a reputation-based technology that uses our Global Intelligence Network to put files in context, using their age, frequency, location and other characteristics to expose emerging threats that might otherwise be missed. If a computer is trying to execute a file that we have never seen anywhere in the world and that comes from an unknown source, there is a high probability that it is malicious—and Insight will either warn the user or block it. SONAR is behavior-based protection that uses proactive local monitoring to identify and block suspicious processes on computers.

Tailoring Security to the Device

Security should also be specific to the device being protected. For example, modern Point of Sale (PoS) systems, which were linked to a number of major data breaches, are at their core just computers running mainstream operating systems. Because a user on such a device typically does not browse the web, send e-mails, or open shared drives, the functionally of the machine and the files that actually need to be on it are limited. This allows businesses to reduce the attack surface by locking down the system and using application control tools, as well as controlling which devices and applications are allowed to access the network. Doing so can render many strains of malware useless because they would not be allowed to run on the devices.

---

[3] *http://www.nist.gov/cyberframework/*

In addition, payment card system infrastructure is highly complex and threats can be introduced at any number of points within the system. Last year we released a report, *Attacks on Point of Sale Systems,* that provides an overview of the methods that attackers may use to gain entry into a system.[4] It also describes the steps that retailers and other organizations can use to protect PoS systems and mitigate the risk of an attack.

Encrypting and Monitoring Data

Encryption also is key to protecting your most valuable data. Even the best security will not stop a determined attacker, and encrypting your sensitive data provides defense in breadth, or across many platforms. Good encryption ensures that any data stolen will be useless to virtually all cybercriminals. The bottom line in computer security is no different from physical security—nothing is perfect. We can make it hard, indeed very hard, for an attacker, but if resourced and persistent criminals want to compromise a particular company or site, with time they are probably going to find a way to do it. Good security means not just doing the utmost to keep them out, but also to recognize that you must take steps to limit any damage they can do should they get in.

Data loss Prevention (DLP) tools are also important in keeping your most valuable data safe and securely on your system. The latest DLP technology allows the user to monitor, protect and manage confidential data wherever it is stored and used—across endpoints, mobile devices, networks, and storage systems. It can help stop the theft of sensitive data by alerting the system manager before the data is exfiltrated, or moved outside the system.

Key Elements for Data Breach Legislation

In the U.S. today, there are at least 48 state-specific data breach notification laws. This creates an enormous compliance burden, particularly for smaller companies, and does little to actually protect consumers. Symantec supports a national standard for data breach notification, built on three principles:

1. *Data security legislation should apply equally to all.* The scope of any legislation should include all entities that collect, maintain, or sell significant numbers of records containing sensitive personal information. Requirements should apply to government and the private sector equally, and should include educational institutions and charitable organizations as well. By the same token, any new legislation should consider existing Federal regulations that govern data breach for some sectors and not create duplicative, additional, or conflicting rules.

2. *Implementing pre-breach security measures should be a part of any legislation.* Breaches are much less costly for companies that are proactive in applying security. New legislation should not simply require notification of consumers in the event of a data breach, but should seek to minimize the likelihood of a breach by pushing organizations to take reasonable security measures to ensure the confidentiality and integrity of sensitive personal information. Numerous standards, best practices, and guidelines already exist to help organizations establish a cybersecurity program or improve an existing one.

3. *The use of encryption or other security measures that render data unreadable and unusable should be a key element in establishing the threshold for the need for notification.* Any notification scheme should minimize ''false positives''—notices to individuals who are later shown *not* to have been impacted by a breach because their data was rendered unusable before it was stolen. A clear reference to the ''usability'' of information should be considered when determining whether notification is required in case of a breach. Promoting the use of encryption as a best practice would significantly reduce the number of ''false positives,'' thus reducing the burden on consumers, businesses, and governments.

Conclusion

Data breaches are continuing at an unprecedented pace, putting consumers at risk and damaging the public's trust in the Internet. While we cannot prevent every cyber attack or every data breach, applying cybersecurity best practices and using risk management principles to protect data appropriately can significantly reduce the attack surface and the impacts we see today. Moreover, legislation cannot stop

---

[4] *Special Report on Attacks on Point of Sale Systems,* Symantec Security Response (February 2014). *http://www.symantec.com/content/en/us/enterprise/media/security\response/whitepap ers/attacks\on\point\of\sale\systems.pdf*

breaches from happening, but smart data breach legislation can help businesses and governments respond effectively and efficiently, and empower consumers with accurate and timely information. At Symantec, we are committed to improving online security and we look forward to continuing to work with government and industry on ways to do so. Thank you again for the opportunity to testify, and I will be happy to answer any questions you may have.

Senator MORAN. Exactly 5 minutes. Thank you very much. Mr. Duncan?

STATEMENT OF MALLORY B. DUNCAN, GENERAL COUNSEL AND SENIOR VICE PRESIDENT, NATIONAL RETAIL FEDERATION

Mr. DUNCAN. Chairman Moran, Ranking Member Blumenthal, members of the Subcommittee, thank you for this opportunity.

Data breaches need to be correctly and forcibly addressed. They fundamentally affect our economy's push toward greater efficiency and cost effectiveness.

By way of context, there is a long history of interception of private communications by individuals and by governments: from steaming open letters to tapping into telephone conversations. Today, we have super computers and the Internet. Together, they are creating a public network with virtually no boundaries, far more versatile and efficient than all the technology that has gone before.

Governments entrust them with critical infrastructure, businesses with their most valuable intellectual property, and millions of people type their deepest secrets into Google, all the while knowing the system is vulnerable to intrusion, both by governments and by sophisticated bad actors.

This interconnected technology is in many ways still in its infancy, having really commercially begun just a quarter century ago. We are still discovering its capabilities, its limitations and risks.

Today, we are here to address one of the most significant risks to emerge—data breach. It is Congress' challenge to incentivize companies to manage this risk in ways that preserve the innovation and benefits this technology clearly offers.

How can Congress do that? There are three essential elements—uniform notice, express preemption, and strong consensus of the laws notice. Let's recognize that data breaches affect everyone.

As the Chairman referenced, in the 2014 Verizon report, retailers suffered their share of breaches, 11 percent. Government agencies incurred a slightly higher percentage. Hotels and restaurants combined constituted 10 percent of breaches, while financial institutions represent 34 percent.

It is not because those with the most breaches have the weakest security. It is because bad actors are always looking for the biggest bang for the buck, and no single set of data security standards is fully protective of any industry.

In a complex economy, each type of business is vulnerable to data breaches in a different way, be it theft of account numbers or Cloud data or intellectual property. Congress needs to provide incentives for companies to increase their security, and nothing motivates like sunlight. Requiring that every company have the same public notice obligations will provide this needed light.

Uniform notice has two benefits. It can help individuals take steps to protect themselves, but equally important, the consequences of requiring all companies to publicly expose their data breaches is a powerful incentive for them to improve security.

NRF members are some of the best known retail companies in America. Recent very public breaches and discussions on how to avoid them have engaged our members' most senior executives. As a result, our members are investing in unique and tailored solutions in an effort to address this ever morphing problem.

Our nation's economy is bigger than retail. Congress needs to encourage disclosure and the incentive for security it brings across the board from all entities that handle sensitive information.

Preemption. There are more than 50 jurisdictions with breach notice laws. Many have common elements but they are not the same. Some cover different datasets, require particular state officials to be notified, and so forth.

Mid-sized companies struggling with the consequences of a breach face a morass of conflicting laws that have become little more than traps for the unwary. In the midst of a breach when a company should be focusing on securing its network and identifying affected customers, they instead divert their limited resources to paying law firms to clear them from regulatory "gotchas."

We need an uniform preemptive Federal law. It would simplify the process for businesses and provide consistent notices for consumers nationwide, but it must be real preemption, otherwise the Federal law just becomes the 52nd set of requirements that companies have to follow, and you will have accomplished worse than nothing.

Finally, it would not be appropriate to preempt the states only to adopt the weakest law. Rather, for a Federal standard, you should be looking well above the median, not the most excessive, perhaps, but language that reflects the strong consensus of the state laws.

We at NRF urge you to go further, establish the same notice obligations for all entities handling sensitive data. Congress should not permit notice holes, situations where some entities are exempt from reporting their known breaches. If we want meaningful incentives to increase security, everyone needs to have skin in the game.

In closing, NRF believes that those three elements, uniform notice, express preemption, and a strong consensus law enforced by Federal authorities and the state AGs, are essential steps to properly and forcibly address the data breach conundrum that is plaguing businesses and consumers.

Thank you.

[The prepared statement of Mr. Duncan follows:]

PREPARED STATEMENT OF MALLORY B. DUNCAN, GENERAL COUNSEL AND SENIOR VICE PRESIDENT, NATIONAL RETAIL FEDERATION

Chairman Moran, Ranking Member Blumenthal, and members of the Subcommittee, on behalf of the National Retail Federation (NRF), I want to thank you for giving us the opportunity to testify at this hearing and provide you with our views on data breach notification legislation and protecting American's sensitive information. NRF is the world's largest retail trade association, representing discount and department stores, home goods and specialty stores, Main Street merchants, grocers, wholesalers, chain restaurants and Internet retailers from the United States and more than 45 countries. Retail is the Nation's largest private sector employer, supporting one in four U.S. jobs—42 million working Americans. Contributing $2.6 trillion to annual GDP, retail is a daily barometer for the Nation's economy.

Collectively, retailers spend billions of dollars safeguarding sensitive customer information and fighting fraud. Data security is something that our members strive to improve every day. Virtually all of the data breaches we've seen in the United States during the past year—from attacks on the networked systems of retailers, entertainment and technology companies that have been prominent in the news, to a reported series of attacks on our largest banks that have received less attention—have been perpetrated by criminals that are breaking the law. All of these companies are victims of these crimes and we should keep that in mind as we explore this topic and public policy initiatives relating to it.

This issue is one that we urge the Committee to examine in a holistic fashion: we need to reduce fraud or other economic harm that may result from a data breach. That is, we should not be satisfied with simply determining what to do after a data breach occurs—that is, who to notify and how to assign liability. Instead, it's important to look at why such breaches occur, and what the perpetrators get out of them, so that we can find ways to reduce and prevent not only the breaches themselves, but the follow-on harm that is often the goal of these events. If breaches become less profitable to criminals, then they will dedicate fewer resources to committing them, and our goals will become more achievable.

With that in mind, these comments are designed to provide some background on data breaches and on fraud, explain how these events impact all business's networked systems, discuss some of the technological advancements retailers have promoted that could improve the security of our networks, offer additional ways to achieve greater payment security, and suggest the elements of data breach notification legislation that may provide the best approach to developing a uniform, nationwide notification standard, based on the strong consensus of state laws, that applies to all businesses that handle sensitive personal information of consumers.

Data Breaches in the United States

Unfortunately, data breaches are a fact of life in the United States, and virtually every part of the U.S. economy and government is being attacked in some way. In its 2014 Data Breach Investigations Report, Verizon determined there were 63,347 data security incidents reported by industry, educational institutions, and governmental entities in 2013, and that 1,367 of those had confirmed data losses. Of those, the financial industry suffered 34 percent, public institutions (including governmental entities) had 12.8 percent, the retail industry had 10.8 percent, and hotels and restaurants combined had 10 percent. *Figure 1* below illustrates where breaches occur.

Where Breaches Occur (Figure 1)

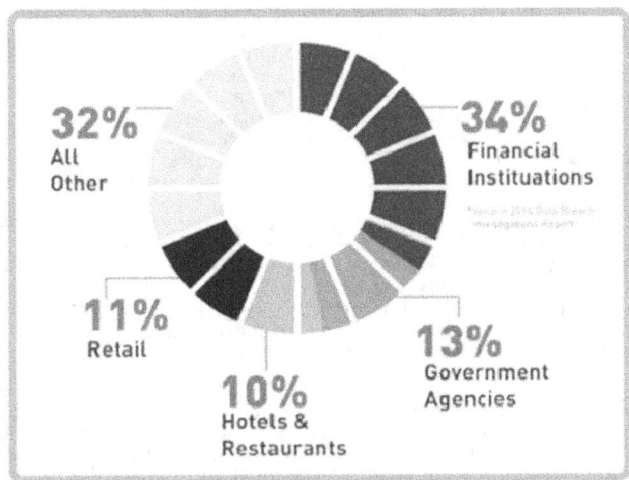

Source: 2014 Data Breach Investigations Report, Verizon[1]

---

[1] 2014 Data Breach Investigations Report by Verizon, available at: *http://www.verizon enterprise.com/DBIR/2014/*

It may be surprising to some, given recent media coverage, that three times more data breaches occur at financial institutions than at retailers. And, it should be noted, even these figures obscure the fact that there are far more merchants that are potential targets of criminals in this area, as there are one thousand times more merchants accepting card payments in the United States than there are financial institutions issuing cards and processing those payments. It is not surprising that the thieves focus far more often on banks, which have our most sensitive financial information—including not just card account numbers but bank account numbers, social security numbers and other identifying data that can be used to steal identities beyond completing some fraudulent transactions.

These figures are sobering. There are far too many breaches. And, breaches are often difficult to detect and carried out in many cases by criminals with real resources behind them. Financially focused crime seems to most often come from organized groups in Eastern Europe rather than state-affiliated actors in China, but the resources are there in both cases. The acute pressure on consumer-serving companies, including those in e-commerce, as well as on our financial system, is due to the overriding criminal goal of financial fraud. We need to recognize that this is a continuous battle against determined fraudsters and be guided by that reality.

Breaches Affect Everyone; Federal Legislation Should Be Similarly Comprehensive

The Year of the Breach, as 2014 has been nicknamed, was replete with news stories about data security incidents that raised concerns for all American consumers and for the businesses with which they frequently interact. Criminals focused on U.S. businesses, including merchants, banks, telecom providers, cloud services providers, technology companies, and others. These criminals devoted substantial resources and expertise to breaching the most advanced data protection systems. Vigilance against these threats is necessary, but we need to focus on the underlying causes of breaches as much as we do on the effects of them.

If there is anything that the recently reported data breaches have taught us, it is that any security gaps left unaddressed will quickly be exploited by criminals. For example, the failure of the payment cards themselves to be secured by anything more sophisticated than an easily-forged signature makes the card numbers particularly attractive to criminals and the cards themselves vulnerable to fraudulent misuse. Likewise, cloud services companies that do not remove data when a customer requests its deletion, leave sensitive information available in cloud storage for thieves to later break in and steal, all while the customer suspects it has long been deleted. Better security at the source of the problem is needed. The protection of Americans' sensitive information is not an issue on which unreasonably limiting comprehensiveness makes any sense.

In fact, the safety of Americans' data is only as secure as the weakest link in the chain of entities that share that data for a multitude of purposes. For instance, when information moves across communications lines—for transmission or processing—or is stored in a "cloud," it would be senseless for legislation to exempt these service providers, if breached, from comparable data security and notification obligations to those that the law would place upon any other entity that suffers a breach. Likewise, data breach legislation should not subject businesses handling the same sensitive customer data to different sets of rules with different penalty regimes, as such a regulatory scheme could lead to inconsistent public notice and enforcement.

Given the breadth of these invasions, if Americans are to be adequately protected and informed, Federal legislation to address these threats must cover all of the types of entities that handle sensitive personal information. Exemptions for particular industry sectors not only ignore the scope of the problem, but create risks criminals can exploit. Equally important, a single Federal law applying to all breached entities would ensure clear, concise and consistent notices to all affected consumers regardless of where they live or where the breach occurs.

Third-Party Exemptions

Figure 2, below, illustrates what some legislative proposals, introduced in the last Congress, would require in terms of notice by third parties. This graphic illustrates a typical payment card transaction in which this Committee has jurisdiction over all of the entities except for the bank. In a typical card transaction, a payment card is swiped at a card-accepting business, such as a retail shop, and the information is transmitted via communications carriers to a data processor, which in turn processes the data and transmits it over communications lines to the branded card network, such as Visa or MasterCard, which in turn processes it and transmits it over communications lines to the card-issuing bank. (Typically there also is an acquirer bank adjacent to the processor in the system, which *figure 2* omits.) Some legislative proposals would only require the retail shop, in this example, to provide notice of a breach of security. The data processor, data transmitter or card company suffering a breach would qualify as a third-party whose only obligation, if breached, is to notify the retail shop of their breach—not affected consumers or the public—so that the retailer provides notice on their behalf. And the bank suffering a breach would be exempt from notifying consumers or the public under most Federal legislative proposals to date. Not only does this notice regime present an inaccurate picture to consumers, but it is fraught with possible over-notification because payment processors and card companies are in a one-to-many relationship with retailers. If the retailers must bear the burden for every other entity in the networked system that suffers a breach, then 100 percent of the notices would come from entities that suffer only 11 percent of the breaches. This is neither fair nor enlightened public policy.

Notice Obligations *Should* Apply to All Breached Entities (Figure 2)

Consumers **need to know when financial data is breached.**

PERCENTAGE OF BREACHES:
34% Financial Institutions
32% All Other
13% Government Agencies
11% Retail
10% Hotels & Restaurants

Obligations to Notify Affected Consumers
NO Obligations to Notify Affected Consumers

A recent example illustrates this point about the risk of over-notifying and confusing American consumers if this proposed third-party notice rule illustrated in *Figure 2* is adopted. The largest payment card breach in history occurred at a payment processor, Heartland Payment Systems, which was breached in 2008 resulting in the compromise of over 130 million payment cards. If Heartland had only followed the proposed third-party notice rule in Federal legislation, rather than notifying the public of its breach (as it did), it would have only been obligated to separately notify each of the merchants that it processed payments for, letting them know the affected card numbers that were breached. Those merchants (who were not breached) would, in turn, have to request (and possibly pay for) the contact information for each cardholder through some arrangement with each affected card company or card-issuing bank, and then make notice to those affected customers and/or make ''substitute'' notice (where individualized notice cannot be made) by announcing the breach to the general public. If affected consumers shopped at a number of retailers that all used the same payment processor that suffered the breach (Heartland, in this hypothetical), the consumers could potentially receive slightly different notices from each store—all providing what they knew about the breach of the same payment processor—when none of those branded retail stores actually suffered the breach itself. This proposal creates an untenable public policy solution that neither serves consumers nor businesses that have secured their own networks.

Just as merchants, such as Target, who have publicly acknowledged a breach have taken tremendous steps to heighten their security, Heartland continued to harden its systems (after notifying of its own breach) and now is recognized as one of the most secure platforms in the industry. The threat of public notice has had a multiplier effect on other commercial businesses.

Indeed, Congress could go further: it could establish the same data breach notice obligations for *all* entities handling sensitive data that suffer a breach of security. Congress should not permit "notice holes"—the situation where certain entities are exempt from reporting known breaches of their own systems. If we want meaningful incentives to increase security, everyone needs to have skin in the game.

Financial Institution Exemptions

Many legislative proposals last Congress, however, had "notice holes," where consumers would not receive disclosures of breaches by certain entities. Perhaps the notice hole that has been left unplugged in most proposals is the exemption from notification standards for entities subject to the Gramm Leach Bliley Act (GLBA), which itself does not contain any statutory language that requires banks to provide notice of their security breaches to affected consumers or the public. Interpretive information security guidelines issued by Federal banking regulators in 2005 did not address this lack of a requirement when it set forth an essentially precatory standard for providing consumer notice in the event banks or credit unions were breached. Rather, the 2005 interagency guidelines state that banks and credit unions "should" conduct an investigation to determine whether consumers are at risk due to the breach and, if they determine there is such a risk, they "should" provide consumer notification of the breach.[2] These guidelines fall short of creating a notification requirement using the language of "shall," an imperative command used in proposed breach notification legislation for entities that would be subject to Federal Trade Commission enforcement. Instead, banks and credit unions are left to make their own determinations about when and whether to inform consumers of a data breach.

Several accounts in 2014 of breaches at the largest U.S. banks demonstrate the lack of any notice requirement under the interagency guidelines. It was reported in news media last Fall that as many as one dozen financial institutions were targeted as part of the same cyber-attack scheme.[3] It is not clear to what extent customers of many of those institutions had their data compromised, nor to our knowledge have the identities of all of the affected institutions been made public The lack of transparency and dearth of information regarding these incidents reflects the fact that banks are not subject to the same requirements to notify affected customers of their own breaches of security as other businesses are required now under 47 state laws and would be required under most proposed Federal legislation, despite the fact that financial institutions hold Americans' most sensitive financial information. A number of the more seasoned and robust state laws, such as California's breach notification law, have not exempted financial institutions from their state's breach notification law because they recognize that banks are not subject to any Federal requirement that says they "shall" notify customers in the event of a breach of security.

Service Provider Exemptions

Another notice hole that has remained unplugged in legislative proposals for many years is the service provider breach exemption, similar to the bank breach exemption, that would permit an entity providing data transmission or storage services to avoid providing consumer or public notice when it is aware of a breach of its data system. Other businesses, such as retailers, are required to provide notice even if they don't have the contact information for the affected consumers. The service provider exemption would, however, permit no notice at all to be made, not even to the FTC or law enforcement for a known breach of security affecting sensitive personal information. Surely Congress should not pass a disclosure law that provides a free pass for known breaches of security to certain service providers simply because they have successfully had such an exemption inserted into some past legislative proposals. Allowing this type of hole in notice requirements does not make sense. Just because a telecommunications provider, cloud data service, payment processor or other company provides a service to another business does not mean it should not have to provide notice of its data breaches. With an exemption for service providers like these, there is real risk that the public won't get information

---

[2] Interagency Guidance on Response Programs for Unauthorized Access to Customer Information and Customer Notice, 70 Fed. Reg. 15736 (Mar. 29, 2005) promulgating 12 C.F.R. Part 30, app. B, Supplement A (OCC); 12 C.F.R. Part 208, app. D–2, Supplement A and Part 225, app. F, Supplement A (Board); 12 C.F.R. Part 364, app. B, Supplement A (FDIC); and 12 C.F.R. Part 570, app. B, Supplement A (OTS), accessible at: *https://www.fdic.gov/news/news/financial/2005/fil2705.html.*

[3] "JP Morgan Hackers Said to Probe 13 Financial Firms," *Bloomberg* (Oct. 9, 2014).

it needs and/or that other businesses will have to plug the gap and take the attendant cost and blame for someone else's data breach. And, of course, such a scheme would not create the incentives for service providers to improve their data security systems.

General Principle for Notification

With respect to establishing a national standard for individual notice in the event of a breach of security at an entity handling sensitive personal information, the only principle that makes sense is that these breached entities should be obligated to notify affected individuals or make public notice when they discover breaches of their own systems. Just as the Federal Trade Commission (FTC) expects there to be reasonable data security standards employed by each business that handles sensitive personal information, a Federal breach notification bill should apply notification standards that "follow the data" and apply to any entity in a networked system that suffers a breach of security when sensitive data is in its custody. With respect to those who have called upon the entity that is "closest to the consumer" to provide the notice, we would suggest that the one-to-many relationships that exist in the payment card system and elsewhere will ultimately risk having multiple entities all notify about the same breach—someone else's breach. This is not the type of transparent disclosure policy that Congress has typically sought. An effort to promote relevant notices should not obscure transparency as to where a breakdown in the system has occurred. Indeed, a public notice obligation on all entities handling sensitive data would create significant incentives for every business that operates in our networked economy to invest in reasonable data security to protect the sensitive data in its custody. By contrast, a Federal law that permits "notice holes" in a networked system of businesses handling the same sensitive personal information—requiring notice of some sectors, while leaving others largely exempt—will unfairly burden the former and unnecessarily betray the public's trust.

More than 50 U.S. Jurisdictions Have Notice Laws; Congress Should Step in Now to Establish a Nationwide, Uniform Standard to Benefit Both Consumers and Businesses

For more than a decade, the U.S. federalist system has enabled every state to develop its own set of disclosure standards for companies suffering a breach of data security and, to date, 47 states and 4 other Federal jurisdictions (including the District of Columbia and Puerto Rico) have enacted varying data breach notification laws. Many of the states have somewhat similar elements in their breach disclosure laws, including definitions of covered entities and covered data, notification triggers, timeliness of notification, provision specifying the manner and method of notification, and enforcement by state attorneys general. But they do not all include the same requirements, as some cover distinctly different types of data sets, some require that particular state officials be notified, and a few have time constraints (although the vast majority of state laws only require notice "without unreasonable delay" or a similar phrase.)

Over the past ten years, businesses such as retailers, to whom all the state and Federal territory disclosure laws have applied, have met the burden of providing notice, even when they did not initially have sufficient information to notify affected individuals, through standardized substitute notification procedures in each state law. However, with an increasingly unwieldy and conflicting patchwork of disclosure laws covering more than 50 U.S. jurisdictions, it is time for Congress to acknowledge that the experimentation in legislation that is at the state level that defines our federalist system has reached its breaking point, and it is time for Congress to the step in to create a national, uniform standard for data moving in interstate commerce in order to ensure uniformity of a Federal act's standards and the consistency of their application across jurisdictions.

For years, NRF has called on Congress to enact a preemptive Federal breach notification law that is modeled upon the strong consensus of existing laws in nearly every state, the District of Columbia, Puerto Rico and other Federal jurisdictions. A single, uniform national standard for notification of consumers affected by a breach of sensitive data would provide simplicity, clarity and certainty to both businesses and consumers alike. Importantly, a single Federal law would permit companies victimized by a criminal hacking to devote greater attention in responding to such an attack to securing their networks, determining the scope of affected data, and identifying the and customers to be notified, rather than diverting limited time and resources to a legal team attempting to reconcile a patchwork of conflicting disclosure standards in over 50 jurisdictions. In sum, passing a Federal breach notification law is a common-sense step that Congress should take now to ensure reasonable and timely notice to consumers while providing clear compliance standards for businesses.

Preemption of state laws and common laws that create differing disclosure standards is never easy, and there is a long history of Supreme Court and other Federal courts ruling that, even when Congress expresses an intent to preempt state laws, limiting the scope of the preemption will not result in preemption. All it will accomplish is to add yet another law, this time federal, to the state statutes and common laws already in effect, resulting in the continuation of a confusing tapestry of state law requirements and enforcement regimes. A Federal act that leaves this in place would undermine the very purpose and effectiveness of the Federal legislation in the first place.

In order to establish a uniform standard, preemptive Federal legislation is necessary. But that does not mean (as some have contended) that the Federal standard must or should be "weaker" than the state laws it would replace. On the contrary, in return for preemption, the Federal law should reflect a strong consensus of the many state laws. Some have called for a more robust notification standard at the Federal level than exists at the state level. Without adding unnecessary bells and whistles, NRF believes that Congress can create a stronger breach notification law by removing the exemptions and closing the types of "notice holes" that exist in several state laws, thereby establishing a breach notification standard that applies to all businesses—as this Committee has done in previous consumer protection legislation that is now Federal law. This approach would enable members that are concerned about preempting state laws to do so with confidence that they have created a more transparent and better notification regime for consumers and businesses alike. It is a way this Committee and Congress can work to enact a law with both robust protection and preemption.

We urge you, therefore, in pursuing enactment of Federal breach notification legislation, to adopt a framework that applies to all entities handling sensitive personal information in order to truly establish uniform, nationwide standards that lead to clear, concise and consistent notices to all affected consumers whenever or wherever a breach occurs. When disclosure standards apply to all businesses that handle sensitive data, it will create the kind of security-maximizing effect that Congress wishes to achieve.

Multi-Tiered Set of Data Security Standards Applicable to Retailers

Theoretically, security is like defense. One could spend all one's money on defense and still not be 100 percent protected. In the real world it is even more difficult.

Federal and State Data Security Standards

Data security standards vary depending on the nature of an entity's business and where it operates. Over the past half-century, the United States has essentially taken a sector-specific approach to data privacy (including data security) requirements, and our current legal framework reflects this. For example, credit reporting agencies, financial institutions, and health care providers, just to name a few regulated sectors, have specific data security standards that flow from laws enacted by Congress, such as the Fair Credit Reporting Act (FCRA), the Gramm-Leach-Bliley Act (GLBA), and the Health Insurance Portability and Accountability Act (HIPAA), respectively. Those operating in other industry sectors that are subject to the jurisdiction of the Federal Trade Commission (FTC) must abide by the standards of care enforced by the FTC under Section 5 of the FTC Act, which give the Commission broad, discretionary authority to prosecute "unfair or deceptive acts or practices" (often referred to as their "UDAP" authority). On top of this Federal statutory and regulatory framework, states have regulated businesses' data security practices across a variety of industry sectors and enforced consumer protection laws through their state consumer protection agencies and/or their attorneys general.

Legal exposure for data security failures is dependent on the Federal or state laws to which a business may be subject and is alleged to violate. The FTC, for example, has been very active in bringing over 50 actions against a range of companies nationwide that are not otherwise subject to a sector-specific Federal data security law (*e.g.*, GLBA, HIPAA, etc.). For example, under its Section 5 UDAP authority, the FTC has brought enforcement actions against entities that the Commission believes fall short in providing "reasonable" data security for personal information. Nearly all of these companies have settled with the FTC, paid fines for their alleged violations (sometimes to the extent of millions of dollars), and agreed to raise their security standards and undergo extensive audits of their practices over the next several decades to ensure that their data security standards are in line with the FTC's order.

Effect of Imposing GLBA-Like Standards with FTC Enforcement

Providing the FTC, however, with the authority to enforce discretionary data security standards like those in the GLBA guidelines would dramatically expand FTC authority. Banking regulators take an audit/examination approach to regulating companies and work with them through an iterative process to help the institution come into compliance where it may be lacking without the threat of severe penalties. The FTC, by contrast, takes an enforcement approach, which under a GLBA guidelines standard, would require a post-hoc determination of a company's compliance with an amorphous standard in a world where the technological threat vectors are ever-changing. In an enforcement approach, entities are either guilty or not, and more often guilty by the mere fact of a breach; unlike with GLBA guidelines, companies regulated by the FTC are not able to get several bites at the apple working with regulators until they know they are in compliance with the regulator's vision for the rule. Companies regulated by the FTC would have to guess at what will satisfy the agency and, if their security is breached, the strong enforcement presumption would be that the company failed to meet the standard.

The different enforcement regimes between financial institutions and entities subject to the FTC's jurisdiction is also evident in the manner and frequency with which fines are assessed and civil penalties imposed for non-compliance with a purported data security standard. Banks are rarely (if ever) fined by their regulators for data security weaknesses. But, as noted, commercial companies have been fined repeatedly by the FTC. Providing an agency like the FTC, with an enforcement approach, a set of standards with significant room for interpretation is likely to lead to punitive actions that are different in kind and effect on entities within the FTC's jurisdiction than the way the standards would be utilized by banking regulators in an examination. A punitive approach to companies already victimized by a crime would not be appropriate nor constructive in light of the fact that the FTC itself has testified before this Committee that no system—even the most protected one money can buy—is ever 100 percent secure.

Improving Payment Card Security

Using the best data security technology and practices available still does not guarantee that a business can avoid suffering a data security breach. Therefore, raising security standards alone may not be the most efficient or effective means of preventing potential harm to consumers. With respect to payment card numbers, for example, it is possible that no matter how much security is applied by a business storing these numbers, the numbers may be stolen from a business's database in a highly sophisticated security breach that can evade even state-of-the-art system security measures. Because of these risks, it makes sense for industry to do more than just apply increased network or database security measures. One sensible proposal is to minimize the storage by businesses of the full set of unredacted and unencrypted payment card numbers necessary to complete a transaction—a data protection principle known as "data minimization." Another method to help prevent downstream fraud from stolen card numbers is to require more data or numbers (such as a 4-digit PIN) from a consumer than simply the numbers that appear on a card to authorize and complete payment card transactions.

For example, a decade ago, the National Retail Federation asked the branded card networks and banks to lift the requirement that retailers store full payment card numbers for all transactions. Retailers have also pushed to phase-out signature-authentication for cards and, instead, use a more secure authentication method for credit and debit card transactions, such as the PIN-based authentication that banks require for accessing bank accounts through ATM machines. PINs can provide an extra layer of security against downstream fraud even if the card numbers (which the card companies already emboss on the outside of a card) are stolen in a breach. In PIN-based transactions, for example, the stored 20-digits from the card would, alone, be insufficient to conduct a fraudulent transaction in a store without the 4-digit PIN known to the consumer and not present on the card itself. These business practice improvements are easier and quicker to implement than any new Federal data security law, and they hold the promise of being more effective at preventing the kind of financial harm that could impact consumers as companies suffer data security breaches affecting payment cards in the future.

On October 17, 2014, the President signed an executive order initiating the BuySecure Initiative for government payment cards.[4] The order provided, among

---

[4] Executive Order—Improving the Security of Consumer Financial Transactions, The White House, October 17, 2014. Accessible at: *http://www.whitehouse.gov/the-press-office/2014/10/17/executive-order-improving-security-consumer-financial-transactions*

other things, that payment cards issued to government employees would include PIN and chip technology and that government equipment to handle and process transactions would be upgraded to allow acceptance of PIN and chip. These are common-sense actions that recognize that while it may not be possible to ensure there is never another data security breach, it is still possible to minimize the harms that can come from those breaches—and reduce the incentives from criminals to try to steal some data in the first place.

PCI-DSS Standards

When it comes to protecting payment card data, however, retailers are essentially at the mercy of the dominant credit card companies. The credit card networks—Visa, MasterCard, American Express, Discover and JCB—are responsible for an organization known as the PCI (which stands for "Payment Card Industry") Data Security Council. PCI establishes data security standards (PCI–DSS) for payment cards. While well-intentioned in concept, these standards have not worked quite as well in practice. They have been inconsistently applied, and their avowed purpose has been significantly altered.

PCI has, in critical respects over time, pushed card security costs onto merchants even when other decisions might have more effectively reduced fraud—or done so at lower cost. For example, retailers have long been required by PCI to encrypt the payment card information that they have. While that is appropriate, PCI has not required financial institutions to be able to accept that data in encrypted form. That means the data often has to be de-encrypted at some point in the process in order for transactions to be processed.

Similarly, merchants are expected to annually demonstrate PCI compliance to the card networks, often at considerable expense, in order to benefit from a promise that the merchants would be relieved of certain fraud inherent in the payment system, which PCI is supposed to prevent. However, certification by the networks as PCI Compliant apparently has not been able to adequately contain the growing fraud and retailers report that the "promise" increasingly has been abrogated or ignored. Unfortunately, as card security expert Avivah Litan of Gartner Research wrote recently, "The PCI (Payment Card Industry) security standard has largely been a failure when you consider its initial purpose and history." [5]

Retailers have spent billions of dollars on card security measures and upgrades to comply with PCI card security requirements, but it hasn't made them immune to data breaches and fraud. The card networks have made those decisions for merchants and the increases in fraud demonstrate that their decisions have not been as effective as they should have been.

Improving Technology Solutions to Better Protect Consumers in Payment Transactions

PIN-Authentication of Cardholders

There are technologies available that could reduce fraud. An overhaul of the fraud-prone cards that are currently used in the U.S. market is long overdue. As I noted, requiring the use of a PIN is one way to reduce fraud. Doing so takes a vulnerable piece of data (the card number) and makes it so that it cannot be used on its own. This ought to happen not only in the brick-and-mortar environment in which a physical card is used but also in the online environment in which the physical card does not have to be used. Many U.S. companies, for example, are exploring the use of a PIN for online purchases. This may help directly with the 90 percent of U.S. fraud which occurs online. It is not happenstance that automated teller machines (ATMs) require the entry of a PIN before dispensing cash. Using the same payment cards for purchases should be just as secure as using them at ATMs.

End-to-End Encryption

Another technological solution that could help deter and prevent data breaches and fraud is encryption. Merchants are already required by PCI standards to encrypt cardholder data but, not everyone in the payments chain is required to be able to accept data in encrypted form. That means that data may need to be de-encrypted at some points in the process. Experts have called for a change to require "end-to-end" (or point-to-point) encryption which is simply a way to describe requiring everyone in the payment-handling chain to accept, hold and transmit the data in encrypted form.

---

[5] "How PCI Failed Target and U.S. Consumers," by Avivah Litan, Gartner Blog Network, Jan. 20, 2014, available at *http://blogs.gartner.com/avivah-litan/2014/01/20/how-pci-failed-target-and-u-s-consumers/.*

According to the September 2009 issue of the Nilson Report "most recent cyberattacks have involved intercepting data in transit from the point of sale to the merchant or acquirer's host, or from that host to the payments network." The reason this often occurs is that "data must be decrypted before being forwarded to a processor or acquirer because Visa, MasterCard, American Express, and Discover networks can't accept encrypted data at this time." [6]

Keeping sensitive data encrypted throughout the payments chain would go a long way to convincing fraudsters that the data is not worth stealing in the first place—at least, not unless they were prepared to go through the arduous task of trying to de-encrypt the data which would be necessary in order to make use of it. Likewise, using PIN-authentication of cardholders now would offer some additional protection against fraud should this decrypted payment data be intercepted by a criminal during its transmission "in the clear."

Tokenization and Mobile Payments

Tokenization is another variant that could be helpful. Tokenization is a system in which sensitive payment card information (such as the account number) is replaced with another piece of data (the "token"). Sensitive payment data could be replaced with a token to represent each specific transaction. Then, if a data breach occurred and the token data were stolen, it could not be used in any other transactions because it was unique to the transaction in question. This technology has been available in the payment card space since at least 2005.[7] Still, tokenization is not a panacea, and it is important that whichever form is adopted be an open standard so that a small number of networks not obtain a competitive advantage, by design, over other payment platforms.

In addition, in some configurations, mobile payments offer the promise of greater security as well. In the mobile setting, consumers won't need to have a physical card—and they certainly won't replicate the security problem of physical cards by embossing their account numbers on the outside of their mobile phones. It should be easy for consumers to enter a PIN or password to use payment technology with their smart phones. Consumers are already used to accessing their phones and a variety of services on them through passwords. Indeed, if we are looking to leapfrog the already aging current technologies, mobile-driven payments may be the answer.

Indeed, as much improved as they are, the proposed chips to be slowly rolled out on U.S. payment cards are essentially dumb computers. Their dynamism makes them significantly more advanced than magstripes, but their sophistication pales in comparison with the common smartphone. Smartphones contain computing powers that could easily enable comparatively state-of-the-art fraud protection technologies. In fact, "the new iPhones sold over the weekend of their release in September 2014 contained 25 times more computing power than the whole world had at its disposal in 1995." [8] Smart phones soon may be nearly ubiquitous, and if their payment platforms are open and competitive, they will only get better.

The dominant card networks have not made all of the technological improvements suggested above to make the cards issued in the United States more resistant to fraud, despite the availability of the technology and their adoption of it in many other developed countries of the world, including Canada, the United Kingdom, and most countries of Western Europe.

In this section, we have merely described some of the solutions available, but the United States isn't using any of them the way that it should be. While everyone in the payments space has a responsibility to do what they can to protect against fraud and data theft, the card networks have arranged the establishment of the data security requirements and yet, in light of the threats, there is much left to be desired.

Legislative Solutions Beyond Breach Notification

In addition to the marketplace and technological solutions suggested above, NRF also supports a range of legislative solutions that we believe would help improve the security of our networked systems, ensure better law enforcement tools to address criminal intrusions, and standardize and streamline the notification process so that consumers may be treated equally across the Nation when it comes to notification of data security breaches.

---

[6] The Nilson Report, Issue 934, Sept. 2009 at 7.

[7] For information on Shift4's 2005 launch of tokenization in the payment card space see *http://www.internetretailer.com/2005/10/13/shift4-launches-security-tool-that-lets-merchants- re-use-credit.*

[8] "The Future of Work: There's an app for that," *The Economist* (Jan. 3, 2015).

Legislation Protecting Consumers' Debit Cards to the Same Extent as Credit Cards

From many consumers' perspective, payment cards are payment cards. As has been often noted, consumers would be surprised to learn that their legal rights, when using a debit card—i.e., their own money—are significantly less than when using other forms of payment, such as a credit card. It would be appropriate if policy makers took steps to ensure that consumers' reasonable expectations were fulfilled, and they received at least the same level of legal protection when using their debit cards as they do when paying with credit.

NRF strongly supports legislation like S. 2200, the "Consumer Debit Card Protection Act," cosponsored by Senators Warner and Kirk last Congress. S. 2200 was a bipartisan solution that would immediately provide liability protection for consumers from debit card fraud to the same extent that they are currently protected from credit card fraud. This is a long overdue correction in the law and one important and productive step Congress could take immediately to protect consumers that use debit cards for payment transactions.

Legislation Protecting Businesses that Voluntarily Share Cyber-Threat Information

In addition, NRF supports the passage by Congress of legislation like H.R. 624, the "Cyber Intelligence Sharing and Protection Act," cosponsored last Congress by Congressmen Rogers and Ruppersberger, and which passed the House of Representatives with bipartisan support. This legislation would protect and create incentives for private entities in the commercial sector to lawfully share information about cyber-threats with other private entities and the Federal government in real-time. This would help companies better defend their own networks from cyber-attacks detected elsewhere by other business.

Legislation Aiding Law Enforcement Investigation and Prosecution of Breaches

We also support legislation that would provide more tools to law enforcement to ensure that unauthorized network intrusions and other criminal data security breaches are thoroughly investigated and prosecuted, and that the criminals that breach our systems to commit fraud with our customers' information are swiftly brought to justice.

Conclusion

In summary, a Federal breach notification law should contain three essential elements:

1. *Uniform Notice:* Breached entities should be obligated to notify affected individuals or make public notice when they discover breaches of their own systems. A Federal law that permits "notice holes" in a networked system of businesses handling the same sensitive personal information—requiring notice of some sectors, while leaving others largely exempt—will unfairly burden the former and unnecessarily betray the public's trust.

2. *Express Preemption of State Law:* A single, uniform national standard for notification of consumers affected by a breach of sensitive data would provide simplicity, clarity and certainty to both businesses and consumers alike. Passing a Federal breach notification law is a common-sense step that Congress should take now to ensure reasonable and timely notice to consumers while providing clear compliance standards for businesses.

3. *Reflect the Strong Consensus of State Laws:* A national standard should reflect the strong consensus of state law provisions. NRF believes that Congress can create a stronger breach notification law by removing the exemptions and closing the types of "notice holes" that exist in several state laws, thereby establishing a breach notification standard that applies to all businesses, similar to the comprehensive approach this Committee has taken in previous consumer protection legislation that is now Federal law.

APPENDIX

What Retailers Want You To Know About Data Security [9]

---

[9] Slides Available at: *http://www.slideshare.net/NationalRetailFederation/thingsto-know-data security?ref=https://nrf.com/media/press-releases/retailers-reiterate-support-federal-data-breach-notification-standard*

ISSUE

Who is breaching?

Cybercriminals are constantly trolling for financial data in order to steal card numbers and convert them into cash.

NRF NATIONAL RETAIL FEDERATION

ABOUT

Where do breaches happen?

Hackers don't discriminate – data breaches have targeted a wide variety of businesses from the entertainment industry to financial services.

According to Verizon, retail represents 11 percent of data breaches while the financial services industry accounts for 34 percent.

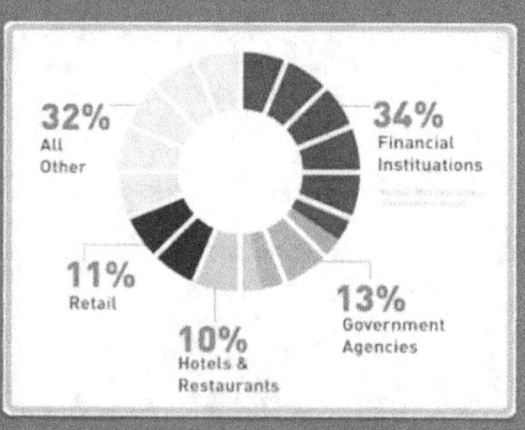

32% All Other

34% Financial Instituations

11% Retail

10% Hotels & Restaurants

13% Government Agencies

NRF NATIONAL RETAIL FEDERATION

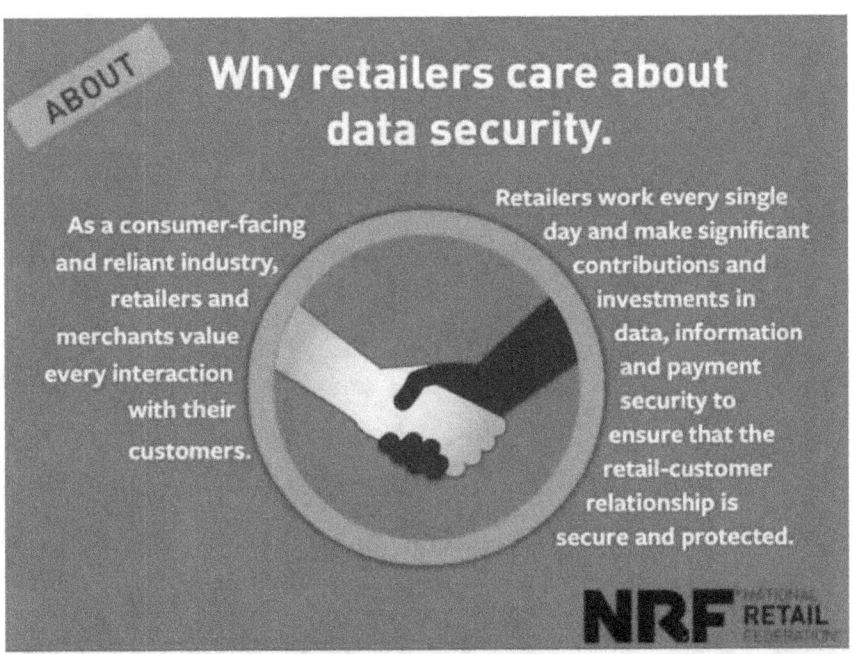

ABOUT

Why retailers care about data security.

As a consumer-facing and reliant industry, retailers and merchants value every interaction with their customers.

Retailers work every single day and make significant contributions and investments in data, information and payment security to ensure that the retail-customer relationship is secure and protected.

NRF NATIONAL RETAIL FEDERATION

PROBLEM

Cards are fraud prone

The thief creates a duplicate card, signs your name and makes a purchase.

The thief uses your card, signs your name and makes a purchase.

NRF NATIONAL RETAIL FEDERATION

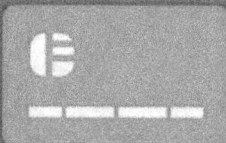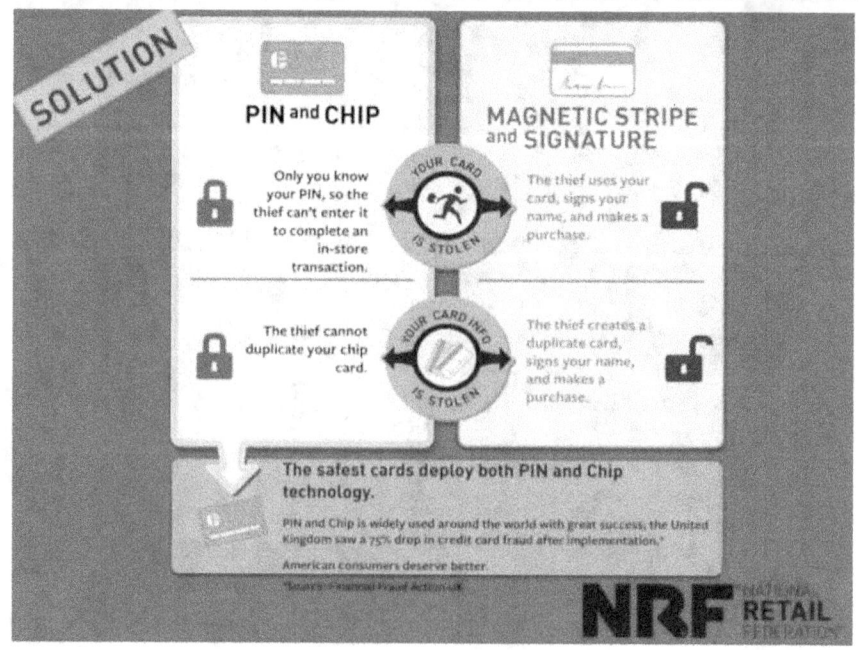

SOLUTION

PIN-and-Chip

Since 2005, the National Retail Federation has urged banks and payment card companies to switch to more secure PIN-and-chip cards, which replace the magnetic stripe with a computer microchip and replace the signature with a Personal Identification Number(PIN) to better protect consumers' financial data when they shop.

The new credit cards being issued this year need to have both a chip and a PIN, not just a chip as proposed by most banks and credit unions. The chip ensures that the card is the one issued by the bank but the PIN is needed to ensure that the person using the card is the actual cardholder and not a thief who stole your chip card.

NRF NATIONAL RETAIL FEDERATION

PROBLEM

Cyber-Threat Information Sharing

Congress must pass laws that make it easier for companies to share information and emerging threats without hesitation.

SOLUTION

NRF's Efforts to Improve Threat Information Sharing

To help fight cybersecurity threats to retailers' systems, NRF created the Information Technology Security Council, which keeps retailers up-to-date on the latest news, information and threats. More than 150 retail companies are actively involved.

PROBLEM

Notification isn't uniform

For the past decade, NRF has called for a uniform nationwide data breach notification standard that would preempt the patchwork of 47 state laws. This uniform federal law should be based on and reflect the strong consensus of state laws.

The current patchwork of state and local data breach notice laws with conflicting requirements doesn't work because it diverts limited resources that should be focused on restoring the integrity of a breached system.

NRF NATIONAL RETAIL FEDERATION

SOLUTION

Data Breach Notification Law

A nationwide breach notification law must preempt state and local laws so businesses and consumers understand what disclosures are expected regardless of when or where breaches occur.

Data breach notification should be appropriate, reasonable, relevant and timely.

Federal data breach notification requirements should be comprehensive and apply to every entity that maintains or transmits sensitive information, not just retailers.

NRF NATIONAL RETAIL FEDERATION

Industries are held to different standards

Merchants have multiple tiers of data security standards. These include Payment Card Industry standards for all merchants accepting payment cards, as well as specific state standards to protect sensitive information. The Federal Trade Commission also enforces federal standards that require all merchants to have reasonable data security protections.

Other breached entities just need to follow industry-specific guidance.

NRF NATIONAL RETAIL FEDERATION

Cover all entities involved in data breach

A data breach notification law should cover the entire payments system from card companies to telecommunications firms without exception or exemption. Arbitrary timeframes or industry-specific requirements that cover only certain entities should not be established.

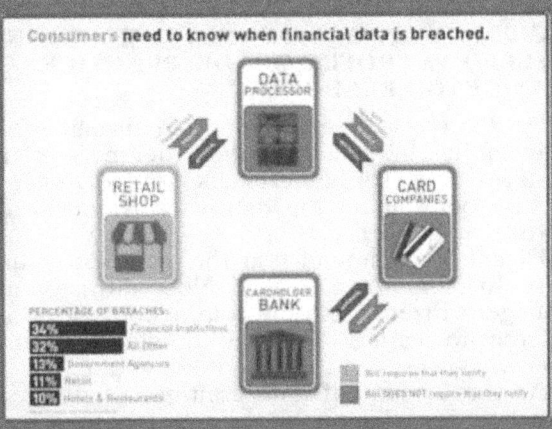

Consumers **need to know when financial data is breached.**

NRF NATIONAL RETAIL FEDERATION

_____

Senator MORAN. Thank you, Mr. Duncan.
Dr. Pendse?

STATEMENT OF RAVI PENDSE, PH.D., VICE PRESIDENT AND CHIEF INFORMATION OFFICER, BROWN UNIVERSITY, CISCO FELLOW, PROFESSOR OF PRACTICE, COMPUTER SCIENCE AND ENGINEERING

Dr. PENDSE. Good morning, Chairman Moran, Ranking Member Blumenthal, and distinguished members of the Committee and my eminent panelists here. Thank you so much for the opportunity to testify today about the data breach and notification legislation. It is truly an honor.

I want to commend you for investing your valuable time to discuss this important area of cyber infrastructure and protection. As younger citizens get online in schools leveraging the power of the Internet to learn and create knowledge, your work on this legislation will be critical to protect our youth.

As the amount of data continues to increase exponentially, primarily driven by our mobile and highly connected lifestyle, your work on this legislation will be critical to protect our ''netizens.''

As Internet connected devices on the ''Internet of Things'' increase in number from 10 billion to a projected 50 billion by 2020, impacting our economy by as much as $19 trillion, according to many experts, your work on this legislation will a critical catalyst to empower connected innovation and wealth generation.

As connected robots and 3D printing fundamentally change how we manufacture goods and manage our supply chain, your work on this legislation will be critical to supporting next generation innovation and our leadership in the world. We are truly looking at some exciting times.

My name is Ravi Pendse. I have the privilege and honor to serve as Vice President and Chief Information Officer at Brown University. I am a Brown University Cisco Fellow and a senior member of IEEE. I am also a faculty member in both computer science and engineering.

My area of expertise and research is in ''Internet of Things,'' cybersecurity, and aviation network security. I take great pride in admitting that I am a nerd.

The Privacy Rights Clearinghouse, as the Chairman pointed out, has reported there have been over 932 million records compromised in over 4,000 plus breaches since 2005.

Just yesterday, as was mentioned, Anthem reported a very large breach, and that breach may impact people in this room since many Federal employees, as I understand, are covered by some of the programs Anthem offers.

We as individuals, organizations, and the Nation must continue to focus in this area for the protection of our consumers and national security.

Currently, 47 states, including Rhode Island, where Brown is located, the District of Columbia, Guam, Puerto Rico, and the Virgin Islands, have enacted data breach legislation. While there are similarities between these state laws, no two are exactly alike.

As a university with students from all 50 states, we are impacted by all of them. Maintaining the necessary standards for each state is challenging and very difficult. This can create a barrier for small innovative organizations lacking the expertise to address the specifics of state laws. In my view, this type of burden will stifle innovation.

Breach notification is a national issue, so I would encourage you to consider a single national legislation. In my view, such legislation should clearly define the rules and actions that are required in the case of a breach. It should identify the methods, speed, delivery, and content of notifications.

A hard time limit for breach notification may be unattainable for small organizations, non-profits, and educational institutions. A tiered approach based upon the size and designation of an organization would make compliance possible for all.

It should also encourage organizations that collect data to be cognizant about the use of such data. Consumers, especially the young ones, appear to be happy to give away their data and their privacy to services, including social media sites, for the sake of convenience.

All acts should clearly define expectations of security for organizations collecting and storing personally identifiable data. Given the highly publicized breaches that have been mentioned, it is apparent that more work is needed. No matter what the size of the company, certain expectations of security should be defined when data is collected and stored.

Most importantly, it should provide incentives to establish education to better combat breaches, so preventive actions are necessary. It is important for us to develop cybersecurity expertise within the U.S. Our national security cannot be offshored.

In conclusion, I applaud your efforts and appreciate the opportunity for this dialogue. I have more details in my written testimony. I stand by to assist you in any way I can. Cybersecurity and cybersecurity education is critical. Our national security cannot be offshored.

Thank you.

[The prepared statement of Dr. Pendse follows:]

PREPARED STATEMENT OF RAVI PENDSE, PH.D., VICE PRESIDENT AND CHIEF INFORMATION OFFICER, BROWN UNIVERSITY, CISCO FELLOW, PROFESSOR OF PRACTICE, COMPUTER SCIENCE AND ENGINEERING

Executive Summary

With an ever-increasing collection of databases, the impact of "big data" on privacy, and the monetary value of personal data used for identity and financial theft, today's America is in need of sound and achievable legislation around data security, privacy, and the notification of consumers after a data breach. Such legislation would benefit all U.S. citizens as well as the organizations collecting and protecting their data.

National legislation governing data breaches will have many advantages over existing state laws and reduce the burden that these dissimilar state laws place on complying organizations. While it's necessary for us to pursue centralized standards, it's important to produce legislation that accommodates organizations of all sizes. In addition to laws regarding data breaches, we should create incentives for proactive measures to reduce the likelihood of breaches, one of the most important being the development of a trained cybersecurity workforce through education and training.

Introduction

Good morning Chairman Moran, Ranking Member Blumenthal, and distinguished Members of the Committee. Thank you so much for the opportunity to testify today about the data breach and notification legislation, it is truly an honor.

I want to commend you for investing your valuable time to discuss this important area of cyberinfrastructure and protection. As younger citizens get online in schools leveraging the power of the Internet to learn and create knowledge, your work on this legislation will be critical to protect our youth. As the amount of data continues to increase exponentially, primarily driven by our mobile and highly connected lifestyle, your work on this legislation will be critical to protect our netizens. As internet-connected devices on the "Internet of Things" increase in number from 10 billion to a projected 50 billion by 2020, impacting our economy by as much as $19 trillion, your work on this legislation will be a critical catalyst to empower connected innovation and wealth generation. As connected robots and 3–D printing fundamentally change how we manufacture goods and manage our supply chain, your work on this legislation will be critical to supporting next-generation innovation and our leadership in the world.

My name is Ravi Pendse. I have the privilege and honor to serve as the Vice President and Chief Information Officer at Brown University. I am a Brown University Cisco Fellow and a senior member of IEEE. I am also a faculty member in both Computer Science and Engineering. My area of expertise and research is in the "Internet of Things", cybersecurity, and aviation network security; I also teach classes in these fields. Currently, I am teaching a class called "Internet of Everything" so your work on this legislation is critical to many young people I interact with each day who I know will change our world for the better.

Thank you again for the opportunity to provide written and verbal testimony relative to a uniform Federal law concerning the definition, protection, and notification of the personally identifiable information of consumers. This is a necessary and extremely relevant topic in our hyper-connected world. The Privacy Rights Clearinghouse reports that there have been over 932,700,000 records compromised in over 4,450 U.S. breaches since April 2005. Countless high-profile security breaches have appeared in the news in the last year. My university witnesses an average of 30,000 attempted attacks each day.

As long as there is a black market for the sale of personal and financial data, and these breaches are attainable, the attacks will continue. At the same time, we are living a mobile and highly connected lifestyle, American children are getting online at a younger age, and ten billion of our household devices are connected to the Internet. This ubiquity of connectivity makes sound security principles and postures a necessity. We, as individuals, enterprises, and a nation, must continue to focus on this area for the protection of our consumers and national security.

Background

Security breach notification laws have been written in most U.S. states since 2002. The first such law, California SB 1386, became the de facto standard for all states nationwide. Since then, other states have been more descriptive in their remedies, making each, in effect, a standard as they appear.

Forty-seven states (including Rhode Island, where Brown is located), the District of Columbia, Guam, Puerto Rico, and the Virgin Islands have enacted legislation requiring private or government entities to notify individuals of security breaches involving personally identifiable information. Many of these state security breach laws have provisions regarding which entities must comply with the law; how "personal information" is defined (such as name combined with Social Security number or driver's license number); what constitutes a breach; how, when, and to whom a notice must be sent; and which situations are exempt (such as a breach of encrypted information). No two are exactly alike.

As a university with students from 49 states, we are impacted by them all. Maintaining the necessary standards for each state has been not only onerous, but also difficult to completely and legally address. This can create a barrier for small, innovative organizations lacking the expertise or legal team to address the specifics of state laws.

Breach notification is a national issue, and the definition of entities, timing, and requirements should not be left to the individual states. Of course, the state Attorney General would have the ability to protect the citizens of their jurisdiction and make claims as such. Having one standard for this conduct would be beneficial to those who protect the information and respond when a security incident occurs.

Recommendations for Cybersecurity Breach Legislation

A single national legislation governing data breaches should be established to replace disparate state laws. This legislation should . . .

1. . . . define the rules and actions that are required in the case of a breach, including the method, speed, delivery, and content of notifications.

2. . . . adjust for the size, nature, and scope of both the breach and the organization. For example, a hard time limit for breach notification may be unattainable for small organizations, nonprofits, and educational institutions without skills in deep forensics and data science. A tiered approach based upon the severity of the breach and size and designation of the organization would make compliance achievable to all.

3. . . . be compliant with current national legislation (such as HIPAA, GLBA, and HITECH) and prevent the possibility of conflict with other Federal laws.

4. . . . mandate that organizations disclose what happens to customer data. Consumers appear to be happy to give away their data (and their privacy) to services including social media sites for the sake of convenience. A requirement to inform consumers how their data and information will be used is a relevant response to this changing landscape of data exchange.

5. . . . define expectations of security for organizations collecting and storing personally identifiable data. Given the highly publicized breaches that have occurred in the past twelve to eighteen months, it is apparent that even many larger enterprises do not provide necessary security. No matter what the size of the company, certain expectations of security should be defined when data is collected and stored.

6. . . . create incentives for the formation of industry forums such as the Financial Services Information Sharing and Analysis Center (FS–ISAC). Such forums provide an opportunity to share threats and approaches within an industry.

7. . . . consider compliance with the accepted framework by the National Institute of Standards and Technology (NIST), or any framework that meets or exceeds the NIST standards, in order to establish the baseline against which to audit.

8. . . . most importantly, provide measures or incentives that establish education to better combat breaches. It is important for us to develop cybersecurity expertise within the U.S.; our national security cannot be offshored. Cisco's 2014 Se-

curity Report estimated a global shortage of more than a million security professionals. While efforts like the National Initiative for Cybersecurity Education (NICE) have attempted to address this shortage, the numbers and expertise of available professionals are still lacking. Cybersecurity programs should be encouraged both in K–12 and higher education. A K–12 program would prepare students to protect themselves as well as join the workforce. Incentives for the expansion of certified cybersecurity programs in higher education, including emerging graduate programs, could make a more immediate impact on the size of the workforce. Similar to the Teach for America program, we could create a conduit for trained security graduates to enter the workforce by establishing a loan forgiveness program dependent upon a designated amount of years in the profession.

Conclusion

We must continue to work on multiple fronts to mitigate the impact of data breaches. Legislation that sets national standards will provide clarity for organizations and balanced protections for all U.S. citizens. As this is a global problem, we must continue to leverage and maximize resources whenever possible to understand and detect persistent threats.

I would be supportive of an effort to create a single, national law around data security and breaches; a national law will remove the undue burden of complying with forty-seven disparate state laws. However, we must be careful to avoid a "one size fits all" model that could be impossible to attain for small organizations, nonprofits, and education. Established tiers of responsibility and compliance levels may better serve all, while legislating a single set of standards that can be embraced and addressed successfully.

In addition to reactive legislation around the handling of data breaches, we need to be proactive. I strongly recommend incentives for proactive measures to reduce the likelihood of breaches, one of the most important being educational initiatives to develop a trained cybersecurity workforce. From additional Americans with forensics expertise to an engaged and educated nation of consumers, we should remember that people provide one of the most critical lines of defense.

Senator MORAN. Doctor, thank you. Good to see you again. Mr. Johnson?

STATEMENT OF DOUG JOHNSON, SENIOR VICE PRESIDENT AND SENIOR ADVISOR FOR RISK MANAGEMENT POLICY, AMERICAN BANKERS ASSOCIATION

Mr. JOHNSON. Yes, good morning, Chairman Moran, Ranking Member Blumenthal, members of the Subcommittee. My name is Doug Johnson, Senior Vice President at the American Bankers Association. I currently lead the Association's physical and cybersecurity business, Continuity and resiliency policy efforts at the Association.

ABA shares the concerns of Congress about protecting consumers in this increasingly sophisticated world of electronic commerce and recordkeeping. It is clear consumers enjoy the efficiency and convenience of conducting transactions electronically.

Notwithstanding these recent breaches, our payment system remains strong and functional, and it is absolutely mandatory that we maintain that trust in the system so that it remains essentially a system that our customers can continue to trust.

While the majority of the transactions are conducted safely, occasional breaches will occur and will continue to occur. Consumers have the right to swift, accurate, and effective notification of these breaches. They also have a right to trust that whenever they conduct business electronically the business is doing everything it can to prevent that the breach is occurring in the first place.

Mr. Duncan mentioned the Verizon study, international sample of private companies and police stations around the world. Other organizations, such as the Identity Theft Resource Center, noted that United States' businesses reported over 30 percent of the reported breaches for 2014, while financial institutions represented 6 percent.

While our numbers may differ and we do believe the United States' numbers are more appropriate to cite, I believe that our intent frankly is the same, and our intent is to ensure that we are protecting customer data, and I think that is essentially both of our goals.

The banking industry supports effective cybersecurity policy and will continue to work with Congress to achieve that goal. Banks are acknowledged leaders in defending against cyber threats. Therefore, from the financial services' perspective, it is critical that legislation takes a balanced approach that builds upon but does not duplicate or undermine what is already in place and effective for the financial sector.

There are three key points that must be considered with regard to data protection standards. First, as others have noted, we do need a national data standard, a data breach standard. Consumer electronic payments are not confined by borders between states. As such, a national standard for data security and breach notification is of paramount importance.

Currently, 46 states, three U.S. territories, and the District of Columbia have enacted laws governing data security in some fashion. Although some of these laws are similar, many have inconsistent and conflicting standards, forcing businesses to comply with multiple regulations and leaving many consumers without proper recourse or protection.

Inconsistent state laws and regulations should be preempted in favor of strong Federal data protection and notification requirements.

Second, any Federal data protection and notification requirement must recognize existing national data protection and notification requirements. Some industries, including financial services, are already required to by law to develop and maintain robust internal protections. They are also required to protect consumer financial information and notify customers when a breach occurs within their systems that would put customers at risk.

We believe the extensive breach reporting requirements currently in place for banks provide an effective basis for any national data breach reporting requirement for businesses generally.

Finally, there must be a strong national data protection requirement associated with any data breach law. All parties must share the responsibility and cost for protecting consumers. The cost of the data breach should ultimately be borne by the entity that incurs the breach.

To limit such breaches, any comprehensive data breach requirement must have strong data protection requirements applicable to any party with access to important consumer financial information.

Thank you, and I will be happy to answer any questions you may have.

[The prepared statement of Mr. Johnson follows:]

PREPARED STATEMENT OF DOUG JOHNSON, SENIOR VICE PRESIDENT AND SENIOR
ADVISOR FOR RISK MANAGEMENT POLICY, AMERICAN BANKERS ASSOCIATION

Chairman Moran, Ranking Member Blumenthal, my name is Doug Johnson, Senior Vice President, payments and cybersecurity policy, of the American Bankers Association. In that capacity, I currently lead the association's physical and cybersecurity, business continuity and resiliency policy and fraud deterrence efforts on behalf of our membership. I appreciate the opportunity to be here to represent the ABA and discuss the importance of instituting a uniform Federal data breach law in place of disparate state laws. The ABA is the voice of the Nation's $15 trillion banking industry, which is composed of small, regional and large banks that together employ more than 2 million people, safeguard $11 trillion in deposits and extend over $8 trillion in loans.

As the 114th Congress engages in public debate on the important issue of data security, we share your concerns about protecting consumers in this increasingly sophisticated world of electronic commerce and record keeping. It is clear that consumers enjoy the efficiency and convenience of conducting transactions electronically. Notwithstanding these recent breaches, our payment system remains strong and functional. No security breach seems to stop the $3 trillion that Americans spend safely and securely each year with their credit and debit cards. And with good reason: Customers can use these cards confidently because their banks protect them from losses by investing in technology to detect and prevent fraud, reissuing cards and absorbing fraud costs. While the vast majority of these transactions are conducted safely, occasional breaches will continue to occur. Consumers have a right to swift, accurate, and effective notification of such breaches. They also have a right to trust that, wherever they transact business electronically, the business is doing everything it can to prevent that breach from occurring in the first place.

The banking industry supports effective cyber security policy and will continue to work with Congress to achieve that goal. Banks are acknowledged leaders in defending against cyber threats. Therefore, from the financial services perspective it is critical that legislation takes a balanced approach that builds upon—but does not duplicate or undermine—what is already in place and highly effective in the financial sector.

In my testimony I will focus on three main points:

- *The value of a national data breach standard.* Consumers' electronic payments are not confined by borders between states. As such, a national standard for data security and breach notification is of paramount importance.

- *The importance of recognizing existing Federal breach requirements.* Any Federal data protection and notification requirement must recognize existing national data protection and notification requirements.

- *The need for strong national data protection requirements.* All parties must share the responsibility, and the costs, for protecting consumers. The costs of a data breach should ultimately be borne by the entity that incurs the breach. To limit such breaches, any comprehensive data breach requirement must have strong data protection requirements applicable to any party with access to important consumer financial information.

I. The Value of a National Data Breach Standard

Our existing national payments system serves hundreds of millions of consumers, retailers, banks, and the economy well. It only stands to reason that such a system functions most effectively when it is governed by a consistent national data breach policy.

Currently, 46 states, three U.S. territories, and the District of Columbia have enacted laws governing data security in some fashion, such as standards for data breach notification and for the safeguarding of consumer information. Although some of these laws are similar, many have inconsistent and conflicting standards, forcing businesses to comply with multiple regulations and leaving many consumers without proper recourse and protection. Inconsistent state laws and regulations should be preempted in favor of strong Federal data protection and notification requirements. In the event of a breach, the public should be informed where it occurred as soon as reasonably possible to allow consumers to protect themselves from fraud.

Given the mobile nature of our Nation's citizens, it is clear that the existing patchwork of state data breach laws are unduly complicated for consumers as well as businesses. For instance, consider a couple residing in a northern state who winter in a southern one and have their credit card data compromised at a merchant in a third state. In this instance, the couple wants to be alerted that their financial data has been compromised and that they are protected. Determining where the couple may or may not reside and which state laws may or may not apply unduly complicates the simple need to protect the couple from financial harm. It also diverts resources at the merchant and the bank toward determining how to comply with a myriad of laws as opposed to fixing the problem.

We believe that the following set of principles should serve as a guide when drafting legislation to provide stronger protection for consumer financial information:

1. Inconsistent state laws and regulations should be preempted in favor of strong Federal data protection and notification standards.

2. Strong national data protection and consumer notification standards with effective enforcement provisions must be part of any comprehensive data security regime, applicable to any party with access to important consumer financial information.

3. Requirements for industries that are already subject to robust data protection and notification requirements must be recognized.

4. In the event of a breach, the public should be informed where it occurred as soon as reasonably possible to allow consumers to protect themselves from fraud. The business with the most direct financial relationship with affected consumers should be able to inform their customers and members about information regarding the breach, including the entity at which the breach occurred.

5. The costs of a data breach should ultimately be borne by the entity that incurs the breach.

II. The Importance of Recognizing Existing Federal Breach Requirements

As we enact a national data breach requirement, some industries—including the financial industry—are already required by law to develop and maintain robust internal protections to combat and address criminal attacks, and are required to protect consumer financial information and notify consumers when a breach occurs within their systems that will put their customers at risk.

Title V of the Gramm-Leach-Bliley Act (GLBA) requires banks to implement a "risk-based" response program to address instances of unauthorized access to cus- tomer information systems. At a minimum, a response program must:

1. Assess the nature and scope of any security incident and identify what customer information systems and customer information may have been accessed or misused;

2. Notify the institution's primary Federal regulator "as soon as possible" about any threats "to sensitive customer information."

3. Notify appropriate law enforcement authorities and file Suspicious Activity Reports in situations involving Federal criminal violations requiring immediate attention;

4. Take appropriate steps to contain the incident to prevent further unauthorized access to or use of customer information, and

5. Notify customers "as soon as possible" if it is determined that misuse of customer information has occurred or is reasonably possible.

A critical component of the GLBA guidelines is customer notification. When a covered financial institution becomes aware of a material breach of "sensitive customer information," it must conduct a reasonable investigation to determine whether the information has been or can be misused. If it determines that misuse of the information "has occurred or is reasonably possible," it must notify affected customers "as soon as possible."

Under GLBA, sensitive customer information includes the customer's name, address or telephone number in conjunction with the customer's Social Security number, driver's license number, credit card, debit card or other account number or personal identification number. Sensitive customer information also includes any combination of components of customer information that would allow someone to log onto or access the customer's account, such as user name and password.

A covered financial institution must also provide a clear and conspicuous notice. The notice must describe the incident in general terms and the type of customer information affected. It must also generally describe the institution's actions to protect the information from further unauthorized access and include a telephone number. The notice also must remind customers to remain vigilant over the next 12 to 24 months and to promptly report incidents of suspected identity theft to the institution.

Where appropriate, the notice also must include:

1. Recommendation to review account statements immediately and report suspicious activity;
2. Description of fraud alerts and how to place them;
3. Recommendation that the customer periodically obtain credit reports and have fraudulent information removed;
4. Explanation of how to receive a free credit report; and
5. Information about the FTC's identity theft guidance for consumers.

We believe the extensive breach reporting requirements currently in place for banks provide an effective basis for any national data breach reporting requirement for businesses generally.

III. The Need for Strong National Data Protection Requirements

Any legislation focused on creating a national standard for breach notification should also include a complementary national data security standard for covered entities. If Congress does not address data security standards now it misses the opportunity to instill a greater overall level of data security protections for consumers.

Every business must share in the responsibility to protect consumers. With that responsibility should come the requirement for that business, whether it be a bank, merchant, third party processor or other entity, to bear the costs for any breach they incur.

To limit the potential for data breaches in the first place, any comprehensive national data breach requirement should be enacted in tandem with strong data protection requirements applicable to any party with access to important consumer financial information. Limiting the potential for such breaches through strong data protection is the first, essential, line of defense in our efforts to maintain customer trust and confidence in the payments system

Effective data protection requirements are scalable. For instance, bank regulations, through GLBA, recognize that the level of risk to customer data varies significantly across banks. Large banks require continual, on-site examination personnel, while community-based institutions are subject to periodic information security examinations.

Data security is also an ongoing process as opposed to the state or condition of controls at a point in time. As opposed to proscribing specific technological security requirements, GLBA and the associated bank regulatory requirements are risk and governance-based. Bank security programs are required to have ''strong board and senior management level support, integration of security activities and controls throughout the organization's business processes, and clear accountability for carrying out security responsibilities.'' [1]

IV. The Path Forward

The legal, regulatory, examination and enforcement regime regarding banks ensures that banks robustly protect American's personal financial information. We believe that this regime provides an appropriate, scalable model for other businesses entrusted with sensitive customer financial and other information.

Senator MORAN. Attorney General Madigan, welcome.

STATEMENT OF HON. LISA MADIGAN, ATTORNEY GENERAL, STATE OF ILLINOIS

Ms. MADIGAN. Thank you, Chairman Moran, Ranking Member Blumenthal, and members of the Subcommittee. I appreciate having an opportunity to testify today.

Data security is one of the biggest challenges that we face as a nation. It is an ongoing struggle for all Americans and the companies, non-profits, and government agencies that hold our personal information.

While last year's massive data breaches reawakened many in the public, breaches are not a new problem. Because of that, 10 years

---

[1] Federal Financial Institution Examination Council IT Handbook, available at *http://ithandbook.ffiec.gov/it-booklets/information-security/introduction/overview.aspx*

ago, I joined 43 other Attorneys General, including at the time Attorneys General Blumenthal and Ayotte, in a bipartisan call for a strong, meaningful national breach notification law, and for over a decade, my office has helped people clean up identity theft damage and investigated major breaches.

In 2005, I drafted Illinois' breach notification law to ensure consumers are told when their personal financial information is compromised, and in 2006, I created an identity theft unit and hotline to help consumers restore their credit when their information was obtained and used without their authorization. So far, we have helped over 37,000 people remove over $27 million worth of fraudulent charges from their credit.

At this point, Americans realize that it is not a matter of if but when they will be a victim of some form of identity theft. The question now is what we do to best assist them to prevent data breaches and reduce identity theft.

First, I want you to recognize that for the most part, we already have data breach notification in this country. As you are aware, 47 states have laws requiring companies to notify people when their personal financial information is compromised. Many states are working to pass their second or third update to their laws in response to the constant threats that are revealed by the almost 4,500 publicly known breaches that have affected over 900 million records since 2005. In this environment, Americans need and expect more transparency of data breaches, not less. Last year, I held over 25 roundtables on data breaches throughout Illinois with nearly 1,000 residents, including local government officials, law enforcement, small business owners, religious leaders, senior citizens, heads of social service agencies, as well as regular consumers.

Here is what they told me. First, they are concerned by the increasing number of breaches and when their information is stolen, they want to know. Second, they want to know what they can do to protect themselves from identity theft. And third, they want to know whether entities are doing enough to prevent breaches and protect their information.

A weak national law that restricts what most state laws have long provided will not meet Americans' increasing expectation that they be told when their information has been stolen. Instead, any definition of ''protected personal information'' should be broad and include the growing types of sensitive information that entities are collecting from individuals, and the FTC should be able to update the definition in response to new threats.

In terms of whether entities are doing enough to protect people's data, unfortunately, as you have already heard from Ms. McGuire and I can tell you from my office's investigations, it has been revealed that entities too often fail to take basic data security precautions.

We have found numerous instances where entities allowed sensitive personal data to be maintained unencrypted, failed to install security patches for known software vulnerabilities, collected sensitive data that was not needed, retained data longer than necessary, and failed to protect against compromised log-in credentials.

Congress should include a provision that requires entities holding sensitive information to take reasonable steps to protect that information.

Next, an entity who suffers a breach should not be conducting a self-serving harm analysis to determine whether consumers get notified about a data breach. Imagine if a landlord learned that a renter's home was robbed and that landlord had the opportunity to decide whether the stolen items were significant enough to let the renter know about the robbery. This is what you will allow when data is stolen with the so-called "harm analysis."

Further, Congress should designate a Federal entity to investigate when massive data breaches that affect millions of Americans, similar to how the NTSB can investigate accidents.

Finally, I know that Congress will consider preempting states' breach notification laws. As a state official, I oppose Federal legislation that limits our ability at the state level to respond to and to safeguard our residents.

If Congress does preempt the states, the preemption provision must be narrow. The law should preserve the states' ability to use their own consumer protection laws and Congress should give the states the right to enforce the Federal law.

I will be happy to answer any questions that you have.

[The prepared statement of Ms. Madigan follows:]

PREPARED STATEMENT OF HON. LISA MADIGAN, ATTORNEY GENERAL,
STATE OF ILLINOIS

Introduction

Chairman Moran, Ranking Member Blumenthal, and members of the Subcommittee, thank you for giving me the opportunity to speak with you. Data security is one of the biggest challenges we face in the United States today. It is an ongoing struggle for companies, non-profits, government agencies, and consumers.

While last year's massive data breaches were a national turning point for public awareness, this is not a new problem. For over a decade, my office has been investigating major data breaches and helping consumers respond to identity theft.[1]

In 2005, we passed a data breach notification law in Illinois to ensure consumers are notified when an entity suffers a breach of their sensitive personal information. And in 2006, I created an Identity Theft Unit and Hotline to help consumers restore their credit when their information was used without their authorization. So far, we have helped remove over $27 million worth of fraudulent charges for over 37,000 Illinois residents.[2]

At this point, everyone knows it is not a question of if they will be a victim of some form of identity theft, but when. Because at every hour of every day, any entity that maintains a database of sensitive information could be under attack.

The economic impacts have been, and will continue to be, enormous. Everyone agrees that we need to do something. Everyone wants to prevent data breaches. And everyone wants to prevent identity theft. The question is—how do we best do this?

I have long supported the push for a national law on data breach notification. In 2005, I joined forty-three other state attorneys general to call for a national law on breach notification,[3] so I am heartened that Congress looks poised to pass a law. But simply passing a law that replicates state laws will do very little to protect consumers that is not already being done.

Congress must move beyond a debate about data breach notification. For the most part, we already have data breach notification in this country. Forty-seven states

---

[1] Since 2006, identity theft and data breaches have either been the most common complaint, or the second most common complaint, received in the Illinois Attorney General's office. Only complaints related to debt have had a higher total.

[2] In 2014, the Illinois Attorney General's office received 2,618 complaints regarding identity theft and helped return over $918,000 to consumers who suffered identity theft.

[3] Letter to Congressional Leaders from the National Association of Attorneys General (NAAG) (Oct. 27, 2005).

have passed laws requiring companies to notify consumers when they suffer data breaches. Many states have either passed, or are working to pass, a second or third-generation version of their laws.

II. The Need for Transparency

We need more transparency on data breaches and data security, not less. We should not hide from the fact that our data can be compromised, and we should not hide data breaches when they occur. I have recently heard an argument that consumers are experiencing data breach fatigue, and that additional notification may be counter-productive. I strongly disagree.

In my experience, consumers may be fatigued over data breaches, but they are not asking to be less informed about them.

Last year, I held over twenty-five roundtables on data breaches throughout Illinois, with nearly 1,000 Illinois residents from all walks of life—law enforcement officials, small business owners, consumers, and senior citizens.

Here is what they told me. When their information is stolen, they want to know. They also want to know what they can do to protect themselves from identity theft and data breaches. And they want to know whether entities are doing enough to protect their information and prevent breaches.

Unfortunately, my office's investigations have revealed that entities have repeatedly failed to take basic data security precautions. We have found instances where entities:

• allowed sensitive personal data to be maintained unencrypted;

• failed to install security patches for known software vulnerabilities;

• collected sensitive data that was not needed;

• retained data longer than necessary; and

• failed to protect against compromised login credentials.

Understanding where data security failures occur is what leads to data security fixes. Without transparency, data breaches and their causes will remain hidden. Notification also allows consumers to take steps to protect themselves following the aftermath of a breach. This transparency is not possible without laws mandating it.

III. Information that Triggers Notification

Therefore, Congress should pass a data breach notification law that covers the growing amount of sensitive personal information that entities are collecting. Any definition of protected "personal information" should be broad, and the Federal Trade Commission should be given the power to update the definition as needed. It is not just stolen social security numbers or stolen credit card numbers that consumers have to worry about now.

When I first worked to pass a law in Illinois on this issue nearly a decade ago, we were focused solely on protecting consumers against identity theft and fraud.[4] In the intervening ten years, the Internet has grown more than we imagined possible. This growth has been great for our economy and it has made our lives easier. But it has also made individuals more vulnerable to data breaches because more entities are collecting increasingly specific data about them. Any law designed to protect consumers should reflect this fact.

Congress should seek to pass legislation that ensures notification of breaches related to pieces of information that can do us any kind of harm, whether that is financial harm or reputational harm. For example, this kind of data includes:

• login credentials for online accounts;

• medical information shared on the Internet that is outside the scope of the Health Information Technology for Economic and Clinical Health (HITECH) Act;[5]

---

[4] Illinois Personal Information Protection Act, 815 ILCS 530/1 et. seq. The Illinois Personal Information Protection Act requires notification to Illinois consumers in the event of a data breach. A breach is the unauthorized acquisition of computerized data that compromises the security, confidentiality, or integrity of "personal information." Currently, "personal information" is defined as an individual's first name (or first initial) and last name combined with any of the following: social security number; driver's license or state identification card number; or account number or credit or debit card number, or an account number or credit card number in combination with any required security code, access code, or password that would permit access to an individual's financial account.

[5] Title XIII of the American Recovery and Reinvestment Act of 2009, Pub. L. 111–5.

- biometric data; and
- geolocation information.

The recent attack on Sony was a lesson for all of us. Reputational harm can be far worse than financial harm. It can hurt companies, and it can destroy lives. In Illinois, I will be seeking to update our law to protect the type of data about individuals that entities are regularly collecting, and I encourage the Subcommittee to do the same.

IV. A "Harm Analysis" Hurts Consumers

Next, an entity should not be conducting a "harm analysis" to determine whether it should notify consumers about a data breach. If an entity holds our sensitive information and loses it, most people want to know. The very loss of sensitive personal information should be viewed as harmful generally, and it is nearly impossible to truly determine what specific harm may or may not occur following a breach.

Imagine if a landlord learned that a renter's home was robbed and that landlord had the opportunity to decide whether the stolen items were significant enough to let the renter know about the robbery. We are considering allowing this for stolen data with a so-called "harm analysis." It will not lead to better data security, only fewer breach notifications.

V. Federal Role in Data Security

Finally, data breach notification alone, no matter how expansive, will not be enough to secure our data. Congress also needs to ensure entities holding sensitive information are taking reasonable steps to protect that information. To do that, it should require companies to implement reasonable security standards and it should give the Federal Trade Commission the authority to promulgate regulations as needed.

Congress should also focus its attention on the current authority of the Federal government to investigate massive data breaches that affect millions of Americans. When such breaches occur, the Federal government should have the general authority to investigate in the same manner the National Transportation Safety Board (NTSB) can investigate accidents. Currently, the Federal government has no such authority. Federal law enforcement agencies can conduct a criminal investigation to determine who was responsible for an attack, and the Federal government, through the Federal Trade Commission and other agencies, can conduct an investigation to determine whether the entity's data security practices were adequate. However, no Federal agency is tasked with simply uncovering what happened in massive data breaches, regardless of whether an entity's data security practices were adequate.

If a Federal agency had this authority, that Federal agency would develop much-needed expertise in data security. It could issue reports about data breaches so that the private sector would better understand what vulnerabilities led to breaches. Our country would also have a much better sense of the general state of our data security.

VI. Role of the States

I understand that Congress will consider preempting states on data breach notification laws. As a state official, I oppose any Federal legislation that limits our ability at the state level to protect our residents. In 2005, along with forty-three other state attorneys general, I wrote to Congress to caution against broad preemption.[6] In the letter, we wrote:

> Preemption interferes with state legislatures' democratic role as laboratories of innovation. The states have been able to respond more quickly to concerns about privacy and identity theft involving personal information, and have enacted laws in these areas years before the Federal government. Indeed, Congress would not be considering the issues of security breach notification and security freeze if it were not for earlier enactment of laws in these areas by innovative states.[7]

In the decade since we wrote that letter, it has become clear that preemption would have been a mistake for consumers.

Additionally, a narrow view of preemption has been adopted in other Federal data security laws. The Gramm-Leach-Bliley Act (GLBA), which established data security

---

[6] Letter to Congressional Leaders from the National Association of Attorneys General (NAAG) (Oct. 27, 2005).
[7] *Id.*

standards for financial institutions, only preempts those state laws that are inconsistent with Federal law and "then only to the extent of the inconsistency." [8]

Similarly, in 2009, Congress took a narrow approach to preemption in the breach notification provisions in the Health Information Technology for Economic and Clinical Health (HITECH) Act.[9] That law imposes the HIPAA preemption standard, which only preempts contrary provisions of state law.[10] For those laws that protect the privacy of individually identifiable health information, the HIPAA Security Rule goes even further, to save any state law that is more stringent than the HIPAA protections.[11] Together, these provisions illustrate a reasonable and workable approach to preemption. If Congress does preempt the states, for the benefit of consumers:

- the law should be a "floor" with a narrow preemption provision;
- the law should preserve a state's ability to use its consumer protection laws to investigate data security practices; and
- states should have the right to enforce the Federal law.

VII. Conclusion

The roundtables on data security that I convened throughout Illinois last year showed me that data breach notification is working. Consumers are well aware of data breaches generally. But one challenge is making sure the affected consumers learn about the right breaches.

Understandably, in certain circumstances, state laws allow companies to comply with notification requirements by notifying the media.[12] Bills being considered in Congress allow similar notification exceptions. But the most often comment I received during these roundtables was that consumers did not know where to go to learn about breaches. It has become clear to me that it is not enough to require companies to notify the media.

As a result, in Illinois, I am proposing a requirement that companies also notify my office when they suffer a breach. Fifteen states already require entities to notify their Attorney General in the event of a breach.[13] If given that authority, I intend to create a website that will enable Illinois residents to see all the breaches that have occurred in Illinois.

Such a website is only possible at the state level because we can include information about national breaches, as well as those that are local or regional. I believe such a service would greatly benefit Illinois residents, and I do not believe they would want Congress to prevent my office from offering it, or the other work we are doing on data security and data breaches.

I am happy to answer any questions you have.

Thank you.

Senator MORAN. Thank you very much. Ms. Weinman?

STATEMENT OF YAEL WEINMAN, VICE PRESIDENT, GLOBAL PRIVACY POLICY AND GENERAL COUNSEL, INFORMATION TECHNOLOGY INDUSTRY COUNCIL (ITI)

Ms. WEINMAN. Thank you, Chairman Moran, Ranking Member Blumenthal, and Senators of the Subcommittee, for the opportunity to testify today.

My name is Yael Weinman, and I am the Vice President for Global Privacy Policy and the General Counsel at the Information Technology Industry Council, known as ITI.

Prior to joining ITI in 2013, I spent more than 10 years at the Federal Trade Commission, most recently as an attorney advisor to Commissioner Julie Brill. I began my career at the FTC in the En-

---

[8] 15 U.S.C. § 6807(a).

[9] Title XIII of the American Recovery and Reinvestment Act of 2009, Pub. L. 111–5.

[10] 42 U.S.C. § 1320(d-7).

[11] 45 C.F.R. § 160.203.

[12] See, e.g., Illinois Personal Information Protection Act, 815 ILCS 530/10(c).

[13] Cal. Civ. Code 1798.29(e); Conn. Ch. 669 Sec. 36a–7041b(b)(2); Fla. Stat. § 501.171(3); Ind. Code Art. 24–4.9–3–1(c); Iowa Senate File 2259 (to be codified at 715C.2.8); LA Admin. Code Title 16 § 701; Maine Stat. Tit. 10 § 1348(5).; Md. Comm. Code § 14–3504(h); Mass. Gen. Law Ch. 93H Sec. 3(a); Mo. Stat. § 407.1500(8); N.H. Ch. 359–C:20(b); N.Y. § 899–aa(8)(a); N.C. Gen. Stat. § 75–65(e1); Vt. Stat. Ann. Tit. 9 § 2435(b)(3); Va. Code § 18.2–186.6(E).

forcement Division, ensuring that companies subject to FTC data security consent orders were in fact complying.

The 59 technology companies that ITI represents are leaders and innovators in the information and communications technology sector.

When consumer information is breached, individuals may be at risk of identity theft or other financial harm. Year after year, identity theft tops the list as the number one complaint reported to the FTC.

Consumers can take steps to protect themselves from identity theft or other financial harm following a data breach. Federal breach notification legislation would put consumers in the best possible position to protect themselves.

I take this opportunity to outline three important principles in connection with Federal data breach notification legislation. First is preemption. A Federal breach notification framework that preempts the existing state and territory breach notification laws provides an opportunity to streamline the notification process.

Complying with 51 laws (47 states, three territories, and one district), each one with its own unique provisions, is complex, and it slows down the notification process to consumers while an organization addresses the nuances in each of these 51 laws.

Complying with 51 different laws also results in notices across the country that are inconsistent and thus confusing to consumers. A Federal breach notification law without state preemption would merely add to the mosaic, resulting in a total of 52 different frameworks.

The second principle is the timing of consumer notifications. An inflexible mandate that would require organizations to notify consumers of a data breach within a prescribed time-frame is counterproductive. Following a breach, there is much to be done. Vulnerabilities must be identified and remedied. The scope of the breach must be determined. Cooperation with law enforcement is imperative, and impacted consumers must be notified. Premature notification could subject organizations to further attack if they have not yet been able to secure their systems, further jeopardizing sensitive personal information.

Premature notification might interfere with law enforcement's efforts to identify the intruders. The hackers might cover their tracks more aggressively upon learning that the breach had been discovered.

Notification to consumers before an organization has identified the full scope of the breach could yield to providing inaccurate and incomplete information.

Organizations have every incentive to notify impacted consumers in a timely manner, but a strict deadline does not afford the necessary flexibility.

The third principle is determining which consumers should be notified. Notifying individuals that their information has been compromised enables them to take protective measures. It is not productive, however, if all data breaches result in notifications.

If inundated with notices, consumers would be unable to determine which ones warrant action. Notifications should be made to consumers if they are at a significant risk of identity theft or financial harm.

A number of factors would be considered in making that determination, including the nature of the breached information as well as whether that information was unreadable. Unreadable information would not warrant a notification. Upon receiving a notice, individuals can then take steps to help avoid being financially damaged.

The three principles I have outlined today are included in the full set of principles that ITI has developed in connection with Federal data breach legislation, and I respectfully request that these be submitted for the record.

2014 has been referred to as ''the year of the data breach,'' and I think many of us would like to see 2015 as the ''year of Federal data breach notification legislation.''

I would be happy to answer any questions. Thank you.

[The prepared statement of Ms. Weinman follows:]

PREPARED STATEMENT OF YAEL WEINMAN, VICE PRESIDENT, GLOBAL PRIVACY POLICY AND GENERAL COUNSEL, INFORMATION TECHNOLOGY INDUSTRY COUNCIL (ITI)

Chairman Moran, Ranking Member Blumenthal, and Senators of the Subcommittee, thank you for the opportunity to testify today. My name is Yael Weinman and I am the Vice President for Global Privacy Policy and the General Counsel at the Information Technology Industry Council, also known as ITI. Prior to joining ITI, I spent more than 10 years as an attorney at the Federal Trade Commission, most recently as an Attorney Advisor to Commissioner Julie Brill.

ITI is the global voice of the technology sector. The 59 companies ITI represents—the majority of whom are based in the United States—are leaders and innovators in the information and communications technology (ICT) sector, including in hardware, software, and services. Our companies are at the forefront developing the technologies to protect our networks. When a data breach occurs, however, we want a streamlined process that helps guide how consumers are informed in cases when there is a significant risk of identity theft or financial harm resulting from the breach of personally identifiable information. In my testimony today, I will focus on several of the critical elements necessary to be considered by Congress in developing a Federal legislative framework for data breach notification in the United States.

''Year of the Breach''

We have all heard 2014 referred to as ''the year of the breach,'' but the reality is that data breaches did not just come on the scene last year—they surfaced quite some time ago. While companies and financial institutions spend tremendous resources to defend their infrastructures and protect their customers' information, it is an ongoing virtual arms race. Organizations race to keep up with hackers while the criminals scheme to stay one step ahead. Unfortunately, it is no longer a matter of *if*, but a matter of *when*, a criminal hacker will target an organization. And when certain information about individuals is exposed, those consumers may be at a significant risk of identity theft or other financial harm. Year after year, identify theft is the number one category of fraud reported to the Federal Trade Commission.[1] I would expect that when the 2014 statistics are released, identity theft will continue to top the list.

51 Different Breach Notification Requirements

As a result of this troubling landscape, over the years, state legislatures across the country enacted data breach notification regimes. Currently, there are 51 such

---

[1] See Federal Trade Commission, Consumer Sentinel Network Data Book for January—December 2013 (February 2014) available at *http://www.ftc.gov/system/files/documents/reports/consumer-sentinel-network-data-book-january-december-2013/sentinel-cy2013.pdf*; and Federal Trade Commission, Consumer Sentinel Network Data Book for January—December 2012 (February 2013) available at *http://www.ftc.gov/sites/default/files/documents/reports/consumer-sentinel-network-data-book-january/sentinel-cy2012.pdf*.

regimes—47 states and four U.S. territories.[2] Consumers across the country have received notifications pursuant to these laws. I have received more than one such notice myself, and I imagine some of you may have as well.

The current scope of legal obligations in the United States following a data breach is complex. Each of the 51 state and territory breach notification laws varies by some degree, and some directly conflict with one another. For example, Kansas requires that notification to consumers "must be made in the most expedient time possible and without unreasonable delay, consistent with the legitimate needs of law enforcement and consistent with any measures necessary to determine the scope of the breach and to restore the reasonable integrity of the computerized data system."[3] Connecticut's notification requirement to consumers is similar, but not identical. It requires notification to "be made without unreasonable delay, subject to [a law enforcement request for delay] and the completion of an investigation . . . to determine the nature and scope of the incident, to identify individuals affected, or to restore the reasonable integrity of the data system."[4] Florida, however, mandates a strict timeline and requires that notification be made to consumers no later than 30 days unless law enforcement requests a delay, regardless of the status of the forensic investigation into the scope of the breach.[5]

The complexities, however, are not limited to the timeline for notification. There are other significant variances among these state and territory laws, including what circumstances give rise to a notification requirement, how notifications should be effectuated, and what information should be included in notifications.

A Way Forward: A Single Uniform Data Breach Notification Standard

Federal data breach notification legislation offers the opportunity to develop a single uniform standard. ITI is currently updating a set of principles that we believe should be reflected in any Federal data breach legislation you consider. I will be happy to share those with you upon their completion, which I expect to be very soon. Outlined below are several of these key policy recommendations.

Consumer Notification

Notifying individuals that their information has been compromised is an important step that then enables them to take protective measures. Notification to consumers, however, is not productive if *all* data breaches result in notifications. If that were the case, consumers would not be able to distinguish between notices and determine which ones warrant them to take action. Notification should be made to consumers if an organization has determined that there is a significant risk of identity theft or financial harm. Upon receipt of such a notice, consumers can then implement measures to help avoid being financially damaged.

The process of determining whether there is a significant risk of identity theft or financial harm will include the examination of a number of factors, including the *nature* of the information exposed and whether it identifies an individual. Accordingly, efforts to define "sensitive personally identifiable information" in legislation should be carefully considered to ensure that over-notification does not ensue as a result of an overly broad definition that includes information, which, if exposed, does not in fact pose a threat of identity theft or financial harm. Determining whether there is a significant risk of identity theft or financial harm may also turn on factors such as whether the information exposed was unreadable. If data is unreadable, its exposure will not result in a risk of financial harm, and therefore notification would not be appropriate.

Consumers will be best served if they are notified not about every data breach, but about those that can cause real financial harm so that they can take precautionary actions only when they are in fact necessary. These actions can often involve expensive and inconvenient measures and should only be borne by consumers when there is a significant risk of identity theft or financial harm.

Timing of Notification

Mandating that companies notify consumers of a data breach within a prescribed time-frame is counterproductive. Recognizing the sophistication of today's hackers, and the challenging nature of the forensic investigation that ensues following the discovery of a breach, Federal legislation must provide a realistic, flexible, and workable time-frame for consumer notification. Companies must be afforded suffi-

---

[2] The District of Columbia, Guam, Puerto Rico, and the U.S. Virgin Islands each adopted a data breach notification law. New Mexico, South Dakota, and Alabama have not yet enacted breach notification laws.
[3] Kan. Stat. § 50–7a02(a).
[4] Conn. Gen Stat. § 36a-701b(b).
[5] Fla. Stat. § 501.171.

cient time to remedy vulnerabilities, determine the scope and extent of any data breach, and cooperate with law enforcement. In certain instances, law enforcement agencies urge organizations to delay consumer notification so that suspected hackers are not alerted and driven off the grid. Sufficient flexibility in the timing of notification allows law enforcement to effectively pursue hackers, and ensures that consumers are neither notified with incomplete or inaccurate information nor notified unnecessarily.

Federal Preemption

A Federal law that preempts the current patchwork of 51 different state laws would provide considerable benefits. A Federal data breach notification requirement without Federal preemption would accomplish nothing other than adding a 52nd law to this patchwork. Federal preemption ensures that consumers will receive consistent notifications, and thus they will be more easily understood. For organizations, it will streamline the notification process, enabling organizations to redirect resources currently being devoted to comply with 51 different notification laws. Such resources can be better utilized following a data breach, which requires a myriad of important steps, including investigating the breach, determining its scope, remedying vulnerabilities, and cooperating with law enforcement. One uniform framework allows organizations to make consistent determinations about who should be notified, when those individuals should be notified, and what information should be included in the notification.

No Private Right of Action

We urge you to avoid legislation that includes a private right of action for violations of a data breach notification regime. The best way to protect consumers is not to empower the plaintiff's bar to pursue actions that are ultimately only tangential to consumer injury. Appropriate government enforcement for violations of data breach notification legislation is the proper remedy.

2015: The Year of Federal Data Breach Notification Legislation

A Federal data breach notification law that preempts the current regime would be an important step forward for 2015—the year after the "year of the breach." At ITI, we hope that 2015 is the "year of a Federal data breach notification law." Thank you again for the opportunity to share our thoughts on a Federal data breach notification regime, and I am happy to answer any questions you may have.

Senator MORAN. Thank you very much, and thank all of our witnesses. Attorney General Madigan, you seem to be in the minority, at least in this panel, on the issue of preemption.

How do you respond to the concern that has been raised particularly by Mr. Duncan or Ms. Weinman about 51/52 different sets of standards across the country? Is there a way to preempt state law but then continue to have states involved in the enforcement of that new standard?

Ms. MADIGAN. Sure. Senator, to answer your second question first, of course, there is—and it happens frequently—at the Federal level, where you will set a national standard but still allow State Attorneys General to enforce the law.

Obviously, if that is what happens, that is one of our most important concerns because there will be instances where there are significant data breaches—they may be smaller, They may be confined to one or only a few states—and it will not be a circumstance where the FTC, for instance, they are the ones with the enforcement authority, will look into it.

In part, it is the same situation we have in terms of different jurisdictions at a State level versus a Federal level, even for criminal matters. Some of the U.S. Attorneys Offices have thresholds. It has to be a big enough matter. But we still need and want the ability, as I said, to respond to and to safeguard our own residents.

In terms of the concern, and I do appreciate having as many as 51 different laws that organizations have to comply with in terms of notification, I would say two things. One, to some extent the concern is overblown, in a very real sense. As somebody mentioned, it is a lawyer that sits down and determines what the notice has got to be and then produces a notice that can be used across the country.

That certainly happened in terms of the Target breach. I remember getting that notification, and there are some different provisions depending on the state, but it is not impossible to do. It does not take such an enormous amount of time that the other issues that need to be contended with during the breach are ignored.

Two, it is not an overall necessity, but I do think it is imperative. And I think everybody agrees that if you set a national standard, it cannot be a weak one. It has to be a higher one than some of the first generation state notification laws because we are seeing an increasing number of breaches with an increasing amount of sensitive information that is being breached.

You are going to have to start to look into biometric data and things that really, during the first generation, very few if any states were concerned about.

Senator MORAN. Thank you very much. Is there any indication, and this is a question for any of the panelists, that from state to state, depending upon the law, that law or the effectiveness of that law has a consequence such that there are fewer hackers?

Is there any suggestion that a state law discourages hacking from taking place in that state? In other words, is it effective as a prevention measure, and is there any suggestion that a state law has increased the standards of businesses who operate in those states?

Is there a different level of compliance and is there a different level of desire to attack in a certain state because of state laws? Mr. Duncan?

Mr. DUNCAN. Senator, as I mentioned in my testimony, the very nature of this problem is that it is interstate. If you imagine a situation with a small startup, they instantly have connectivity throughout the entire United States if they are selling merchandise. It is the fact of notice regardless of which state it occurs in that drives the interest in trying to have greater standards. It is not really a state issue. This is a national problem.

Senator MORAN. We often think of the states as laboratories, and I assume if we develop a national standard that we will look at states to see what standards are there, what makes sense.

I just wanted to make certain there was no suggestion that a particular state has found a way to prevent or discourage this kind of behavior. I think at least your answer, Mr. Duncan, is no.

Mr. Johnson?

Mr. JOHNSON. Yes, sir. I would echo that the answer is no. I think what it does is it points to the need to have really a data security standard that is attentive to any data breach standard. If you do not have both pieces, you really do not have the ability to raise the bar from a security standpoint, because I do not believe that a breach notification in and of itself motivates businesses to essentially raise the cybersecurity bar.

Senator MORAN. Thank you, Mr. Johnson. Let me ask you before my time expires, is there any developing insurance coverage market for data breach? Your banks have a standard in place today. Is there insurance that covers the consequences of a data breach?

Mr. JOHNSON. Yes, there is. It is a maturing market. We actually have a captive insurance company that offers some of those policies as well. I think it is a market that needs further refinement.

We as an industry are looking at that very carefully in a number of different fashions, and in fact working with Treasury and with the Administration generally to try to figure out ways to improve the market and try to build insurance as a private incentive as opposed to building public incentives toward greater cybersecurity.

Senator MORAN. Thank you. Senator Blumenthal?

Senator BLUMENTHAL. Thanks, Mr. Chairman. Ms. Madigan, again, thank you for being here. I want to follow up on a couple of questions that the Chairman asked.

You make the point that preemption has sometimes been narrow in our laws. In fact, that concept of narrow protection is that there should be preemption only if state laws are inconsistent with Federal law and then only to the extent of the inconsistency. That is a quote from one of those statutes.

In Gramm-Leach-Bliley, in the Health Information Technology for Economic and Clinical Health Act, also known as HITECH, that principle of narrow preemption has been adopted.

Has the experience been with that narrow approach to preemption that there are these horrible inconsistencies or confusion that our witnesses seem to raise as a specter of avoiding preemption?

Ms. MADIGAN. No, Senator. The concern from the state level, as you are aware, is that it took—let's assume Congress will pass something this year—it took 10 years for Congress to pass a breach notification law, if you pass it now.

To the extent that there are new threats out there or, again, threats that specifically target a group of people, consumers in our state, we need to be able to respond. Or, if there is a rapidly changing area, again, we want to be able to respond.

I think that is the real concern. We have not seen significant problems where states retain enforcement authority of a Federal law and/or the preemption is narrow. In fact, I think it works best that way because, again, Federal resources tend to go to larger issues whereas state resources go to some of the smaller issues.

Senator BLUMENTHAL. Mr. Duncan, I am troubled by the failure of retailers to take responsible steps to protect their consumers. In fact, some of them, I am told, have actually blocked some of the new technology that could have been available. I do not want to call any out, but I am happy to name them if you wish.

I am disturbed that these major retailers have in fact moved to block innovations by disabling their contact list transaction terminals that they offered as a feature to consumers for many years. Mobile payment technologies like Apple Pay and Google Wallet, efforts are underway, but they still have not been deployed as they should be.

Are you not disappointed that retailers have not done more to protect their consumers?

Mr. DUNCAN. It is not a matter of disappointment in terms of what retailers have done in the past. I can tell you that I have sat in the Board meetings of the National Retail Federation, and I have heard the CEOs of some of the best known companies in this country talk long and seriously about the steps they have to take to address this very serious problem.

Senator BLUMENTHAL. I am sure they have talked about it. Why have they not done anything about it?

Mr. DUNCAN. They are also adopting new technologies. This is a very complicated issue to address because there are so many ways, as has been pointed out, that the bad actors can get in, so you have to develop very particularized systems that will effectively block that, and they are adopting those.

Senator BLUMENTHAL. Why are the retailers disabling their terminals, for example?

Mr. DUNCAN. There are some technologies that either are unproven, are extraordinarily expensive, or take control of the company's operations away from the company and into someone else's. Each company has to make its own decision on that element, but that is completely separate from a decision about how you secure the data in your files.

Senator BLUMENTHAL. You know, I am struck that you have recommended to the panel that there be preemption, not only of state statutory law but also common law. That is a pretty broad preemption, is it not?

Mr. DUNCAN. The fact is if you do not have preemption that is strong and across the board, then ultimately, experience has shown us, that the courts will strike down the preemption and the proliferation of conflicting laws will reemerge. We have to have a very strong law and it has to be an uniform law if it is to be effective.

Senator BLUMENTHAL. That principle of preemption, is that not virtually unprecedented?

Mr. DUNCAN. No, I do not think so.

Senator BLUMENTHAL. Where else has it been adopted?

Mr. DUNCAN. Well, let's look at what has happened with the telemarketing sales rule that the FTC enforces. There essentially the same kind of approach was taken. All power was placed essentially on the rule with the FTC. You do not see individual actions under that rule or you do not see——

Senator BLUMENTHAL. My time is expired.

Mr. DUNCAN. State Attorneys General actions under that rule, which we would support.

Senator BLUMENTHAL. My time has expired. I would suggest that that approach to preemption is broader than this committee should consider, and a more narrow view of preemption such as Attorney General Madigan has suggested, if there is to be any preemption at all, is one that is more appropriate.

Thank you, Mr. Chairman.

Senator MORAN. Thank you, Senator Blumenthal. Senator Fischer?

STATEMENT OF HON. DEB FISCHER, U.S. SENATOR FROM NEBRASKA

Senator FISCHER. Thank you, Mr. Chairman. My thanks to you and the Ranking Member for holding this very timely hearing today.

Ms. McGuire, as you know, numerous reports have linked nation state actors to cyber attacks. Additionally, some of the same countries implicated in these reports may require U.S. IT companies to turn over intellectual property, including operating software source code, in exchange for market access.

Are you concerned that such information in the hands of what we could call an ''irresponsible actor'' could pose additional cybersecurity risks?

Ms. McGUIRE. Thank you for the question. We are concerned about having to turn over any of our intellectual property to any country. We believe that is an infringement on our ownership of our intellectual property that we have clearly spent extensive resources to develop, and that we should be allowed to protect it accordingly.

Certainly, if it is passed to a third party or a second party, then it does expose us to potential additional vulnerabilities. In short, we believe that we should not have to share our intellectual property.

Senator FISCHER. There are instances, I believe, where companies are being pressured by foreign governments to share that property. Do you know how prevalent that is?

Ms. McGUIRE. There are some new requirements, actually some not so new requirements, in some countries. I cannot tell you how prevalent it is, but we are certainly seeing a growth in those kinds of requests from many different countries around the world.

Senator FISCHER. How dangerous is that if we continue to see growth in that, that companies do that for increase in market access, for example? How dangerous is that to other companies here in our country when that property is shared, would it not put your security and other companies' security at risk?

Ms. McGUIRE. It potentially could put other organizations at risk. I am not sure I can quantify how much, but any time you have to provide the source code to another party, it can provide additional openings for risk.

Senator FISCHER. Also, our Federal data protection framework, it is largely based on who is collecting that information rather than tailoring enforcement based on what is being collected. Would it not be better for consumers and businesses alike if we would apply a more uniform regime for all entities so that enforcement is based on the sensitivity of the information that is being collected?

Ms. McGUIRE. Yes, that is our view, that it should be a risk-based application and threshold for what type of data potentially is breached.

Senator FISCHER. For all the witnesses, if I could just ask a couple of yes or no questions here. Do you support a Federal data breach notification standard that is consistent for all consumers? Ms. McGuire, if you want to start.

Ms. McGUIRE. Yes.

Mr. DUNCAN. Absolutely.

Dr. PENDSE. Yes.

Mr. JOHNSON. Yes.

Ms. MADIGAN. Yes, if it is strong and meaningful.

Ms. WEINMAN. I will be the outlier and ask for further clarification of the question. When you say ''consumers,'' are you referring

52

to which particular type of data? Is that your question, whether you do not want to distinguish between types of data?

I think to a certain extent the sectoral approach that we have here in the United States has worked to a large extent with regard to financial data and health data.

Since the desire is to get Federal breach notification legislation across the finish line in 2015, anything that could potentially slow that down is something we should carefully consider.

Senator FISCHER. Do you think it would be easier to get something across the finish line if exceptions are made or targeting made on what type of data is collected?

Ms. WEINMAN. I think it would make it easier to get it across the finish line if entities that are already subject to data breach notification requirements in specialized areas—if those remain intact.

Mr. DUNCAN. Senator Fischer, with all due respect, a sectoral specific approach or exceptions are anathema to the kind of incentives we are going to need in order to have effective protection for consumers, at least in the view of the National Retail Federation.

Senator FISCHER. So, we have disagreement. I am over my time, so thank you very much.

Senator MORAN. Senator Schatz?

STATEMENT OF HON. BRIAN SCHATZ, U.S. SENATOR FROM HAWAII

Senator SCHATZ. Thank you. Ms. Weinman, you and others have talked about the balance to strike in terms of over-notification. I think we all recognize we do not want to be inundating consumers and others with notification of breaches if they are not significant enough, and it would become meaningless.

My question is who determines whether there is this "significant risk" of identity theft? Do you figure that gets enshrined in the statute? Is that for Attorneys General to determine? Is it the courts? Individual companies?

I think that is one of the key issues here. We can all agree in principle that we do not want to be over notifying, but where that responsibility and authority resides is really key.

Ms. WEINMAN. Thank you. I am glad that we can all agree in principle that over notification is not something that would be desirable. I think an organization that holds the data and has a sense of what information has been compromised, and the extent to which it had been compromised, would be in the best position to make that determination.

Senator SCHATZ. What standard would they be held to? Would it be under the law or just their own judgment about whether this was going to be harmful to their consumers? Or does this all get refereed in court? That is the question, is it not?

Ms. WEINMAN. Well, I think the level of risk would be something that would be codified in a statute like significant risk of identity theft or financial harm. I do think that would be in the letter of the law.

Senator SCHATZ. Ms. McGuire, you were talking about a risk-based analysis. I would like you to elaborate there.

Ms. McGUIRE. So, along the same lines of what kind of data has been breached and what the risk is to the consumer or the organizations that also might have been part of that, but as I stated in my statement, we believe that a component of that statute needs to be that the data has been either rendered unreadable or unusable via encryption or other technologies so that in fact if the data has been accessed, it is meaningless to the perpetrator. That is a key component——

Senator SCHATZ. That is your bright line?

Ms. MCGUIRE. Of the statute; yes.

Senator SCHATZ. Attorney General Madigan, maybe take half a minute to elaborate on that, and I have another question for you as well.

Ms. MADIGAN. I do not think there is any such thing as over notification going on at this point. Notification keeps consumers alert to the possibility of I.D. theft and they should be protecting themselves.

It certainly depends on what other information these criminals may have access to in terms of what they could be using; information that we would deem individually not to pose any risk to them, but could potentially if it is combined with other information. There is no over notification going on at this point.

Senator SCHATZ. I agree with you there may not be over-notification but we do not want to create a scenario where I am getting e-mails two or three times a week and I do not know what to panic about and what to ignore. I think that is the balance to strike.

I agree that we are not there in reality.

Ms. MADIGAN. At all.

Senator SCHATZ. If you could again articulate what would constitute a sufficiently strong standard to kind of satisfy your concerns. I respect the California law and some other statutes are pretty good marks to make. I see a few heads nodding, I see a few heads shaking.

Ms. MADIGAN. Do not scare them.

Senator SCHATZ. That is fine. I would like to hear what you think would suffice in terms of being worth a tradeoff in terms of pre-empting state laws.

Ms. MADIGAN. I think a strategy that I have heard talked about here is that you really should look at the state laws that are out there, California probably at this point being one of the high marks. But I should say it is not just California. Again, this is a bipartisan issue: Texas, Florida, Indiana, have some of the most progressive notification laws in the country.

You need to look and see what the changes have been from the first generation of them, such as Illinois, where we said it is going to be your first name or your first initial and your last name along with unencrypted Social Security number, driver's license number, credit or debit card number, and now we are moving to biometric data, as I said, and e-mail addresses with log-in passwords.

As it changes, you really need to look and see what is the high water mark and make sure that really is your floor.

Senator SCHATZ. Mr. Johnson, I will let you have the last word on this. What would suffice as a strong enough standard that we would all feel comfortable preempting the 50 odd state laws that we would be looking at?

Mr. JOHNSON. Gramm-Leach-Bliley.

Senator SCHATZ. I'm sorry, one more time.

Mr. JOHNSON. Gramm-Leach-Bliley, the Federal law. I think what we are doing at the Federal level has a standard associated with when a company makes a valuation, such as your concern in terms of who has the responsibility to make the determination as to when to notify of substantial harm.

I think also the financial services companies even if a breach is not occurring at the financial services company has a lot of experience in terms of dealing with those breaches as well, and they look at Gramm-Leach-Bliley from that perspective. I think that is what I would look to.

Senator SCHATZ. Thank you.

Senator MORAN. Senator Blunt?

STATEMENT OF HON. ROY BLUNT,
U.S. SENATOR FROM MISSOURI

Senator BLUNT. Thank you, Chairman. Thank you for having this hearing. We had a similar hearing in this committee last March, and at that time all the panelists were for a single, consistent national standard.

Attorney General Madigan, I often tend to be in favor of the underdog, but I seldom would imagine you would be the underdog on this issue. You might be in terms of where other people are tending to wind up.

I think a lot of the questions I would ask have already been asked on the topic of preemption. We will just see where that goes. The President and the Attorney General have both taken a position, and both agree with the need for preemption.

Senator Carper and I introduced a bill last year, and we are working on a bill again this year. Our bill covers a lot of ground regarding data security and breach notification, but one of the things we have not done in our legislation is establish an arbitrary timeframe.

There is an argument about whether there should be a specific timeframe established in the law as opposed to established by circumstances. So far I have stayed on the side that we need to have some flexibility in timeframes, but I am not absolutely sure I understand, or the Committee understands, all of the reasons why.

I did notice in the Anthem data breach this week, they sent a general notice, and then I heard Mr. Schatz say basically he was becoming the victim of breach fatigue by being constantly notified that he could be in a group whose information may have been breached.

I have not yet looked at legislation with the idea that we need an arbitrary deadline, but I have a couple of questions for whoever wants to answer, starting with you, Ms. Weinman.

The question would be what would you perceive in terms of how a deadline should be established or the criteria for what would be a reasonable response, and your view on whether an arbitrary deadline is something that should be included in a data breach notification.

Ms. WEINMAN. Thank you. I think an arbitrary deadline, a specific timeframe, is not useful in that it sets an objective standard. Each data breach incident is different. Each incident requires special consideration to address vulnerabilities, and to cooperate with law enforcement. Some breaches will require cooperating with many different types of law enforcement.

I do not think a specific deadline is useful. That being said, a number of the states have deadlines that do not involve specific days, and I think that is the right approach to give sufficient flexibility.

Senator BLUNT. Is there any sort of guidelines you would look at as to whether or not a response was appropriate, and made in an appropriate timeframe? What would be a triggering factor of whether the response was appropriately quick or not?

Ms. WEINMAN. I think the buzz words that we hear a lot is "without unreasonable delay," that type of construct, I think, works well in this situation. In examining whether the notification was done without unreasonable delay, you would look at what the company had done up until that point when it decided to make that notification.

Had they dotted all the i's and crossed all the t's and closed the patches, cooperated with law enforcement, listened to law enforcement if law enforcement asked them to in fact delay notification, which is in fact sometimes the case.

Senator BLUNT. I am down to a minute. Anybody that feels a guideline should be specific? Anybody want to respond to that?

Ms. McGUIRE. I do not, and I agree with Ms. Weinman that there should be a standard for reasonable notification, but I think it is important to recognize that there are different types of breaches. There is a difference between losing a laptop that has a lot of data on it and a network that has been penetrated. That may require very different responses and very different investigation and time lines. I think that is an important criteria to consider.

Dr. PENDSE. I would agree with my colleagues here, there ought to be some flexibility there because smaller organizations are simply not going to have the types of resources that bigger organizations can bring to bear, so some flexibility would be very much essential.

Senator BLUNT. Anybody? I think I am out of time. I am not a lawyer but it does sound like—my one concern about "reasonable response" is it sounds like time in court to me for someone to try to determine whether the response was reasonable or not.

I am out of time. Chairman, thank you for the time.

Senator MORAN. Thank you, Senator Blunt. We are honored to be joined by Chairman Thune, and I recognize him now.

STATEMENT OF HON. JOHN THUNE,
U.S. SENATOR FROM SOUTH DAKOTA

The CHAIRMAN. Thank you, Mr. Chairman. I thank you and Senator Blumenthal for holding this hearing and focusing a light on this issue. It is an issue that is important to our country and something that Congress has been trying to fix for over a decade, and hopefully this will be the year when we finally find the path forward that enables us to put in place a workable solution that protects consumers and addresses this very important issue, which again we are reading about today, millions of Americans impacted by yet another data breach.

I want to ask, and Senator Blunt mentioned this, because I think the question has been asked many times but perhaps not everyone has answered it, Ms. Weinman, I am just curious because you have extensive experience in this area having worked at the FTC prior to your current position with ITI, could you give us your sort of explanation of why you think a single Federal law is so preferable for both businesses and consumers?

Ms. WEINMAN. Thank you. I have a chart with me that is 19 pages long that goes through the variances of the different state laws. That reason alone, I think, lends itself to having one Federal breach notification standard to enable companies to act quickly and provide the required notice. I think it is both business-friendly but more importantly consumer-friendly.

The CHAIRMAN. Mr. Duncan, your testimony today highlighted the need for Congress to enact a preemptive Federal data breach notification law. I agree that doing so would provide a great deal of clarity for companies, including the retailers and merchants that you count as your members.

It also would provide needed consistency, I think, for consumers. That is an issue as I said before Congress has dealt with in the past. There has been various legislative proposals that have called not only for uniform notification procedures but also for uniform Federal data security standards.

I appreciate your observations about some of the risks of FTC enforcement, but since that enforcement can already occur, would not retailers benefit from a Federal law saying that reasonable data security measures must take into account the size and scope of the organization and the sensitivity of the data collected?

Mr. DUNCAN. Thank you, Senator Thune. The FTC effectively has a reasonableness standard either under exception or under unfairness right now.

Once you begin putting a lot of different factors into that standard, then you essentially set up a situation where was it reasonable as to (a), as to (b), as to (c), as to (d). If a medium-sized company cannot check the box on every single one of those factors, then they are likely to be in very bad shape.

That kind of standard works better when you are developing guidance. That is a big distinction between the GLB standards that Mr. Johnson has talked about, and a uniform national standard.

If you have an examiner sitting next to you, and you—can in an iterative process—work through each of those various elements, that may work. If you are trying to set one standard for every type of commerce and every type of business in the country, then having multiple components to that is going to make it impossible with any certainty for the average American company to respond to.

The CHAIRMAN. Could NRF support any type of security requirement?

Mr. DUNCAN. Sure, if there is a standard comparable to that the FTC is currently enforcing, which is a reasonable security standard, and if that is coupled with the very, very robust notice requirements that we have testified in favor of, that would work.

The CHAIRMAN. I have a question for Attorney General Madigan. Ms. McGuire in her testimony suggests that any notification standard should minimize notifying individuals about breaches in which their personal information was rendered unusable before it was stolen.

Ms. Weinman suggests that the exposure of unreadable data will not result in risk, therefore, notice would not be appropriate.

I am wondering what your thoughts are on the wisdom of including the usability reference in breach notice legislation and then perhaps how the Illinois state law approaches that issue.

Ms. MADIGAN. It is the right thing to do. I agree with both of them on that front. Under Illinois' law, if the information is encrypted, you do not get notification of the breach. What we need to look to, because we have seen this in some of the breaches taking place, is encrypted information that has been compromised and the encryption key has also been stolen.

In those circumstances, when you can unencrypt, then there should be notice. If it is encrypted—if it is unusable, unreadable—notification does not need to take place under Illinois law.

The CHAIRMAN. Great. Mr. Chairman, thank you.

Senator MORAN. Mr. Chairman, thank you. Senator Klobuchar?

STATEMENT OF HON. AMY KLOBUCHAR, U.S. SENATOR FROM MINNESOTA

Senator KLOBUCHAR. Thank you very much, Mr. Chairman. Thank you for holding this important hearing. I apologize for being late. We had a Judiciary markup. It was very exciting. Now I am here on a topic that is near and dear to our hearts in Minnesota.

As you know, one of our major retailers experienced a breach, and I think there is not a day that goes by that we do not hear about another cyber attack in local communities or on the national scene or even on the international scene.

In fact, last night the media reported that Anthem, the nation's second largest health insurer, was breached, and as many as 80 million customers could have had their account information, including names, birth dates, addresses, Social Security numbers stolen.

These cyber attacks are increasing in scope. I was a sponsor of some of the bills that were out there in the last Congress. I hope, given that we have already had hearings this Congress, and I appreciate Senator Thune's leadership—I am one of the few senators that are on both the Judiciary Committee and the Commerce Committee—that we can move ahead in this area of cybersecurity.

My first question actually was about what I just raised, and I know it was in the news. Attorney General Madigan, welcome. I have worked with you in the past and appreciate your good work.

With this disclosure, it is important to discuss what is and what is not covered under the Health Insurance Portability and Accountability Act or HIPAA. To your knowledge, would the information impacted in the Anthem breach be covered by HIPAA?

Ms. MADIGAN. What I have heard so far is that they claimed medical information was not breached, so it probably falls under the various state breach notification laws to determine if the "personal information" definition is met at the various states. I think it remains to be seen what the total extent of that breach is.

Senator KLOBUCHAR. I know. I do not think we know yet. In your experience when something like this happens, not this exact case, how are the agencies coordinating with the Attorneys General, whether it is the Department of Health and Human Services, or the FTC, to enforce these consumer protections, and do you think there is more that can be done there when it comes to coordination?

Ms. MADIGAN. Well, we have certainly had a very good working relationship with the FTC because we obviously have similar jurisdiction over consumer matters. We probably do not have as much interaction with the other entities that are dealing with some of the health information, but in Illinois, the way our breach notification law works, if that type of information is taken, we want the ability to be able to make sure people are notified. And obviously, coordination, I think, helps everybody, particularly when we all have limited resources.

At the end of the day, our concern is all the same, right? We are trying to protect individuals from any sort of identity theft and financial damage that could occur because of it. We are always looking to cooperate, whether it is at the state level or at the state and Federal level.

Senator KLOBUCHAR. OK. Mr. Duncan, I am going to focus on the retail issues, since we are proud to have Target and Best Buy in the State of Minnesota, two great companies.

Last year, many of my colleagues and the media had talked about the need to move to chip-and-PIN technology, similar to what we are seeing in Europe, Canada, and elsewhere, and following the push for the change, the industry made a voluntary commitment, as you know, to switch over to chip-and-PIN cards and readers by the end of October 2015, which is this year.

That is an important timeline, I think, for consumers. We learned from the Home Depot data breach that impacted both Canadians and Americans that cards from Canada were actually less valuable on the black market than American cards because they had chip-and-PIN technology. We tended to be a target because we had not improved that technology, despite the work of companies like Target who had early on tried to, but as we know, it is not universal across the country.

Mr. Duncan, what percentage of your members have already adopted chip-and-PIN payment technology and have the necessary technology to read cards at points of sale?

Mr. DUNCAN. This is a quickly changing number. I have data from several months ago, in which case it was in excess of a quarter of the Nation's retail terminals were already outfitted for chip-and-PIN.

The concern that many of our members have is that the investment in PIN-and-chip technology is extraordinarily expensive. It will cost between $25 and $30 billion to re-terminalize the entire country.

It is worth it if you get improvement in fraud reduction. Unfortunately, many of the banks, not all, but many of the banks are not issuing pin and chip cards. They are only issuing chip and signature cards. As you know, a signature is a virtually worthless security device.

Retailers are being asked to spend tens of billions of dollars for security that is going to be illusory.

Senator KLOBUCHAR. I know just talking to Target and Best Buy that they are pretty committed to getting to this October deadline, which is great. When you are talking about the 25 percent, those are just ones that have not done it yet but you expect a higher percentage to be there by October?

Mr. DUNCAN. Lots of companies—it takes a huge effort to re-terminalize a large operation, an interconnected operation. We expect a significant portion of the industry to be there, not 100 percent. It is impossible to do that in 10 months.

Senator KLOBUCHAR. Your point is it is very important to have the full technology with the chip-and-PIN and——

Mr. DUNCAN. If we are going to spend the money to reduce fraud, let's reduce fraud. Let's do PIN-and-chip.

Senator KLOBUCHAR. Any comments from anyone else about this? Mr. Johnson? Thank you, Mr. Duncan.

Mr. JOHNSON. Thanks for the opportunity, Senator. I think one of the things when we have this conversation that we forget sometimes is the fact that the card market is really two different markets to some degree. It is the debit card market as well as the credit card market. Debit cards have PINs. You essentially have more than 50 percent of the card environment already that is PIN enabled.

What we have learned from the credit side is the fact that both at the retail side as well as our customer behavior, in the credit environment, our customers prefer to use the signature. If they want to be protected by a PIN, they can use their debit cards. They have an effective choice to be able to really accomplish that.

Senator KLOBUCHAR. I think what Mr. Duncan said is that you get more protection, and certainly the situation that we saw with Home Depot where the Canadian cards were less valuable because they had that full technology, I can imagine everyone would like to see. It is just that if we know one technology protects better, it seems we would not just want it for debit cards.

Sometimes, I just know from having a bunch of cards in my purse, I do not really think through what kind of card it is, if it is signature or not.

Mr. JOHNSON. I think that the most important thing here is to really work toward getting rid of static numbers. What we have in the environment right now are credit card numbers and PINs that are static numbers that make us vulnerable.

To the extent that we have developed technologies such as tokenization, where numbers are meaningless, if someone was to breach Target and capture all the numbers that were associated with those transactions, or any retailer, the numbers would be meaningless because they would only work for that one transaction.

I think that is really what we need to be working toward, making those numbers absolutely worthless to the criminal, and that is what is really going to protect the customer at the end of the day.

Senator KLOBUCHAR. Very good. The last thing, just for the good of my hometown, Target did fix the breach and everyone can go shopping there. Thank you.

Senator MORAN. Thank you. Senator Daines. Let me first say that a vote is scheduled at 11:30. I want to make sure that Senator Daines gets an opportunity to question. We intended to take a second round, but that may not be possible based on the voting schedule. Senator Daines?

STATEMENT OF HON. STEVE DAINES, U.S. SENATOR FROM MONTANA

Senator DAINES. Thank you, Mr. Chairman. This morning, 80 million Anthem health insurance customers woke up to learn their personal identifiable information could have been stolen. In fact, we just received this over the fax machine, a notice from Anthem that says ''To our Members,'' and I am just quoting from the letter which was sent out to their members, and it could be 80 million members.

''These attackers gained unauthorized access to Anthem's IT system and have obtained personal information from our current and former members, such as their names, their birthdays, their medical I.D.'s, Social Security numbers, street addresses, e-mail addresses, and employment information, including income data.''

Last year in the House I offered an amendment that would strengthen victim notification requirements. I am eager to work with the chairman on strengthening these requirements again in future legislation.

I have a question for anyone on the panel here this morning in light of there has been a lot of discussion about past breaches and now we have this most recent significant and most serious breach.

What is an appropriate notification time period, like for these 80 million customers, and we still do not know for sure when this occurred, but we are hearing it might have been last week, but for these 80 million customers that are waking up this morning to hear and learn their PII could have been stolen.

Ms. MADIGAN. Senator, I would respond this way. It sounds unusual and helpful that Anthem has actually notified people, even if we do not know the full extent of the breach, as quickly as they have.

We are aware of situations where there are retailers who have waited months and months, some maybe as long as six months, to notify people, which is clearly too long to notify.

We have had some extensive discussion about whether there should be a 30-day hard deadline, should it be more flexible. I can tell you at the state level, while there are some that have time-frames, we have been very reasonable, basically saying to do this as expeditiously as possible.

When we look into whether that has taken place, we determine when did the breach take place, when did the company know about it, did they have time to put in place a response to secure their system, and obviously, any exceptions, if they need to continue to work with law enforcement.

A flexible deadline would be a good one, but it cannot be that there is such a flexible deadline that you never have to notify or that you can wait for months, because your goal is to let people know that their information is out there and they may be a victim of some form of financial fraud or identity theft.

Senator DAINES. Prior to coming up on the Hill, I spent 28 years in business, in fact, half of that time at Procter & Gamble. We prided ourselves on good customer service. The other half of that time as part of a technology startup, a Cloud competing company that we took public. In fact, Oracle acquired us a couple of years ago, built a world class Cloud competing company.

I was the Vice President of Customer Service working with literally millions of end users and thousands of customers. We sold a B to C customer service Cloud-based solution.

When I was running Customer Service and looking after customers and we had a problem, our policy was we notified our customers as soon as we were aware of the problem, maybe not always understanding the magnitude of it. We believed we owed it to our customers to get back to them.

I frankly am surprised to think we might be thinking in terms of 30 days. I think frankly that is unacceptable and that the customers, the consumers in this country, should be served better than that, and particularly when we are dealing with PII, recognizing we may not know the scope of the problem at the time, but at least the customers ought to know there is a problem and we are working quickly here to try to resolve that.

I would be happy if there are any other comments from the panel.

Mr. DUNCAN. Senator, we would support the kind of a notice regime that is contained within the Illinois law. It is less important as to what the number of days are attached to it, as long as you provide the time for law enforcement, for example.

They may not want to notify because they want to set a trap for the people who have invaded it and have a way of catching them, taking them off the street. You have to allow for that.

You clearly want to clean up the holes so that the people cannot come back inside. Once you have taken care of that, 30 days, 10 days, whatever, 40 days, it does not matter, just a reasonable time period.

I will say to the specific point that was made a moment ago, one of our members had a breach which they initially interpreted to be a million card data's that had been released. Once they examined it, it turned out there were only 35,000.

The idea that you would have given notices to 965,000 more people unnecessarily is a pretty serious problem. You have to get it right. There is no easy answer here.

Dr. PENDSE. If I may comment, in terms of customer service, I agree with you that quick notification is very important but on the other hand a serious situation such as my other panelists have pointed out, some flexibility is necessary.

One of the biggest detriments to any organization is loss of trust. As we noticed, Anthem has been very quick at reaching out to people and hopefully they will learn from past challenges and also from other well publicized breaches that have occurred.

Loss of trust is a very big detriment and in the current environment, in an Internet enabled information gathering session, people have to quickly respond.

Senator DAINES. I would hope to continue to work on this issue of trying to establish what we think would be without unreasonable delay and trying to perhaps put better guardrails on that. I think it is probably in the eyes of the beholder sometimes.

With my experience of years of working in a Cloud-based competing company, I just believe it is better to err on the side of the consumer and their protection. I fully understand the fact you can create maybe a bigger problem by notifying everybody without understanding what really has happened.

I think as we lean one way or the other on this, I would just urge us to lean toward a quicker response, defining that. I think it is kind of better safe than sorry, particularly looking at this notification that went out, this is Social Security numbers, this is personal income data, this is perhaps private medical records. This is very, very serious.

I think the consumer has the right to know about that sooner than perhaps waiting a week as we try to walk the fine line here of law enforcement and not creating a mountain out of a mole hill.

I will tell you what, I think we should be trying to make this tighter. I had 2 days with an amendment I offered, and I hope we can work on something here that we can actually define.

Senator MORAN. Senator Daines, thank you very much. The bell has rung indicating votes. We will conclude this meeting momentarily.

I am not going to ask any additional questions, but Dr. Pendse, I would be glad to have you visit with my staff. You know Kansas well. What small businesses should we be worried about? What innovators may be deterred from greater innovation as a result of this kind of legislation? I would welcome your input.

Dr. PENDSE. Absolutely.

Senator MORAN. I would be interested in hearing from any of the witnesses about Gramm-Leach-Bliley and its potential being used as a standard.

I would like to know with the bankers, if there is information that banks have that could be breached that is not covered by Gramm-Leach-Bliley, and also the same kind of question related to HIPAA, where in those two arenas, health care and financial services, is there something we ought to be considering, a standard, or a starting point as we look at broader breach opportunities, or is that just a bad idea.

Senator Blumenthal, anything to add?

Senator BLUMENTHAL. Yes, I agree with you that Gramm-Leach-Bliley offers a potential model here. Mr. Johnson, I am quoting from your testimony, ''The extensive breach reporting requirements currently in place for banks provide an effective basis for any national data breach reporting requirement for businesses generally.''

I gather that you support the preemption model that is contained in Gramm-Leach-Bliley.

Mr. JOHNSON. That is correct.

Senator BLUMENTHAL. Because I think that may provide some common ground here. I invite the witnesses—I apologize, my time expired before, Mr. Duncan, you may have been able to provide a full answer to my question, so I would invite you to supplement your answer in writing if you wish, because I value your further comments.

Thank you, Mr. Chairman.

Mr. DUNCAN. If I may, Senator Blumenthal, I would emphasize the fact that Gramm-Leach-Bliley is essentially guidance. It is precatory language. It says you should, you ought to, something like that. That differs quite a bit from the state laws that have a mandate and a requirement.

We would favor a mandate and a requirement rather than something that is merely precatory.

Senator BLUMENTHAL. I was referring really to the preemption model there.

Senator MORAN. Senator Klobuchar had exceeded her time at the earlier opportunity.

Senator KLOBUCHAR. Oh, new kid on the block.

[Laughter.]

Senator MORAN. Senator Blunt, any concluding comments?

Senator BLUNT. In the great tradition of Senators, that is what we are expected to do. I think actually Senator Daines has followed up on the question that I had, but I want to ask one more time.

Mr. Duncan a couple of different times has established a matrix of what might go into a reasonable standard. Is there anyone on the panel who is concerned about the Congress pursuing, as we look at this issue, a reasonable standard sort of along the lines that have been outlined as opposed to a specific notification period?

Ms. MADIGAN. Are we talking about timeframe?

Senator BLUNT. We are. Nobody is proposing that we should include a specific timeframe in any law that we require notification in.

Ms. MADIGAN. Senator, what I can tell you is the reasonable timeframe such as what Illinois has, we have seen it abused. The idea is that you would put in a specific deadline: within the most expedient time, but in no circumstances less than, put some sort of a line there. Or, as I said, it could be 6 months, at which point your information is long gone. It has long been purchased on the black market, and who knows what has been done with it or what damage has been done to you.

You need to have further discussions about how do you try to better define what the time line is going to be for notification.

Senator BLUNT. Anyone else?

[No response.]

Senator BLUNT. Thank you.

Senator MORAN. Thank you, Senator Blunt. To be bipartisan in my admonition, Senator Daines also exceeded his time allotment. I also note that Senator Klobuchar was very effective in putting me in my place by saying something like "the new kid on the block."

Senator KLOBUCHAR. Yes.

[Laughter.]

Senator MORAN. We are delighted you all were here. We appreciate the information that was conveyed to us.

The hearing record will remain open for two weeks. During that time, Senators are asked to submit any questions for the record.

Upon receipt of those questions, the witnesses are requested to respond to the Committee as soon as possible.

I thank the witnesses again for their testimony, and I conclude this hearing. We are adjourned. Thank you.

[Whereupon, at 11:39 a.m., the hearing was adjourned.]

APPENDIX

PREPARED STATEMENT OF STEPHEN ORFEI, GENERAL MANAGER, PAYMENT CARD INDUSTRY SECURITY STANDARDS COUNCIL

The Payment Card Industry Security Standards Council (PCI Council) thanks you for this opportunity to offer our insights toward national legislation on data security and breach notification.

The PCI Council is an open global forum that is responsible for the development, management, education, and awareness of the PCI security standards, including the Data Security Standard (PCI DSS), Payment Application Data Security Standard (PA–DSS), and PIN Transaction Security (PTS) requirements. Founded in 2006, the PCI Council has 700 participating organizations representing merchants, banks, processors, and vendors worldwide. Our mission of helping all stakeholders in the payment card industry prevent breaches involving sensitive payment data is led by the multi-industry leadership organization that exists to keep the payment system safe. With our global collaboration of security stakeholders, the PCI Council has created and maintains robust data security standards designed to prevent breaches and keep consumers' data safe. As part of these efforts, our organization regularly engages stakeholders with certification programs, training courses and best practice guidelines to help them meet new threats and improve continuous processes required for securing payment card data.

Because PCI is the global forum for managing PCI security standards, we are uniquely qualified to address the need for a security standard in national data breach and notification legislation.

The complexity of computer, networking and electronic payment technology offers tremendous opportunity for consumers, but also creates an attractive opportunity for criminals to exploit vulnerabilities in software and hardware. As we have seen in the recent past, errors in system configurations, weak passwords, malicious actions by insiders, or simple mistakes by anyone connected to sensitive payment card data can lead to infiltration of networks that lead to data breaches. At the PCI Council, we believe security results from the right combination of people, processes and technology. There is no silver bullet to protecting data, but instead it takes a multi-layered approach to prevent breaches. Technical standards are but the first step toward achieving data security.

We believe the Committee is correct in addressing the important need for data security. The good news is that many security standards already exist, are widely implemented at least on a partial basis, and undergo regular enhancement to meet evolving threats. For example, the National Institute of Standards and Technology's (NIST) Special Publication 800–53 and other related standards are crucial for Federal data security. The International Standard Organization's ISO 27000 family of security standards are used globally. The PCI Council's portfolio of security standards for the global payment industry is another example. The PCI DSS is our over-arching data security standard, collaboratively built on 12 principles that cover everything from implanting strong access control, monitoring and testing networks, to having an information security policy. All of these standards mentioned share many common elements.

We urge the Committee to avoid recreating the wheel or conflicting with existing security standards, and instead leverage the invaluable work that is already used by organizations as practical frameworks for data security.

It is true that despite the existence of security standards, criminals have successfully breached some databases and stolen sensitive data. But in the majority of cases, forensic investigations show breaches are preventable—and result from improper implementation of security standards. For example, in recent prominent retail breaches, attackers used a relatively simple technique of inserting malware onto vulnerable back-office computers, which then infiltrated points-of-sale to steal payment card data. Breaches like these could have been prevented by following prescriptions of security standards—such as frequently scanning internal systems for out-of-date, unprotected software and correcting those configurations. Cases like these also illustrate why the PCI Council urges deployment and vigilant ongoing monitoring of a wide range of best practice security technologies used as "defense in depth" to backstop protection against unpredictable threats.

With the ever evolving vectors of attack, businesses cannot assume that passing a compliance evaluation at a point in the past will protect their data in the future. Attackers are persistent and their threats continue to evolve. Businesses must take prudent and reasonable steps to keep their data security protocols up to date. This is true whatever standard is used.

The PCI Council is deeply committed to helping payment card industry stakeholders meet evolving threats and vigilantly defend payment card data. As an example, the PCI Council welcomes the North American payment industry's migration to "EMV Chip" technology, and recognizes that transactions companies have been working towards the adoption of EMV since 2011. The presence of an identifying integrated circuit chip in each payment card will significantly reduce fraud in card-present transactions. Based on global experience with EMV, we know that after the U.S. transitions to this technology, fraud will migrate to the card-not-present environment such as online or over the phone. Accordingly, the best defense for protecting payment card data is a multi-layered combination of EMV Chip and new technologies that take sensitive account data out of harm's way, coupled with implementing PCI standards.

The new technologies, including encryption and tokenization, are intended to "devalue" stolen payment card data throughout the payment system by scrambling the sensitive data and making it unusable to a data thief. Making systemic changes like these take time and investment while technologies are in their infancy, however, so until then, organizations that store, transmit or process payment card data must be vigilant 24/7 in monitoring their implementations of PCI standards.

The Committee's work will help bolster our stakeholders' vigilance by having the Federal government facilitate sharing security information with the private sector. We are encouraged by the possibility of other deterrents to data breaches such as increasing penalties for cybercrimes, and negotiating cybercrime treaties with key foreign nations.

The PCI Council welcomes the opportunity to work with the Committee and Congress as it considers emerging data security, breach notification, cybersecurity and privacy legislation.

RESPONSE TO WRITTEN QUESTIONS SUBMITTED BY HON. ROY BLUNT TO
CHERI F. MCGUIRE

Question 1. Today, there are 51 different laws dealing with breach notification, and another 12 dealing with security requirements—with even more states considering new laws, or changing their existing laws.

Given this trend, do you think Federal data breach legislation should include a clear national standard for both data security and breach notification?

Answer. Yes. A clear national standard would provide clarity for consumers, businesses, and advocacy groups. In the current environment, organizations have to comply with myriad and sometimes conflicting standards. This adds cost and complexity for the organizations, and can lead to confusion among consumers because they can receive multiple—but different—notifications after a breach. This serves no one's interest. A Federal standard should apply equally to the private sector and the government—it should cover all entities that collect, maintain, or sell significant numbers of records containing sensitive personal information. It should also seek to minimize the likelihood of a breach by pushing organizations to take reasonable security measures to ensure the confidentiality and integrity of sensitive personal information. This would also lower the cost of an event as studies have shown that breaches are less costly for companies that were proactive in applying security. Finally, any notification scheme should recognize that state-of-the-art encryption renders data unreadable, which in turn will minimize "false positives"– notices to individuals who are later shown not to have been impacted by a breach because their data was rendered unusable before it was stolen.

Question 2. Do you think the 51 different breach notification laws create confusion for consumers—especially for those who move, travel frequently, or live in an area where they shop and work across state lines?

Answer. Yes. As noted above, existing standards can proscribe different forms of notices and require notification in different situations. As a result, a consumer could receive multiple, different breach notices from one company, or hear conflicting reports as to whether a breach actually happened because the standard was met in one state but not in another. Breaches and risk of identity and credit card theft are confusing enough as it is; no one is served by conflicting rules and laws that send mixed messages to potential victims.

———

RESPONSE TO WRITTEN QUESTIONS SUBMITTED BY HON. ROY BLUNT TO MALLORY B. DUNCAN

Question 1. Today, there are 51 different laws dealing with breach notification, and another 12 dealing with security requirements—with even more states considering new laws, or changing their existing laws.

Given this trend, do you think Federal data breach legislation should include a clear national standard for both data security and breach notification?

Answer. The Federal Trade Commission (FTC) enforces a general reasonableness standard with respect to data security within the confines of the existing "unfair" and "deceptive" prongs of Section 5 of the FTC Act. The commission's unfair and deceptive standards have worked for commercial law enforcement because they are broad enough to encompass an array of businesses and practices, and because they are implemented through the commission's consent decree authority—which allows for the clarification of requirements over time, without unduly penalizing businesses exposed to novel or developing requirements.

If section 5 were amended to include a comparably broad requirement to maintain "reasonable data security," without more, and were coupled with existing cease and desist enforcement authority, it would have a similarly positive effect of advancing data security without exposing them to penalties for unanticipated, evolving risks. If this were also coupled with the very robust notice requirements that we have testified in favor of, that would be something that might work well.

Conversely, if the legislation were to establish a multi-factor data security standard—similar in nature to the Gramm-Leach-Bliley Act (GLBA) data security guidelines—for businesses which are subject to FTC jurisdiction, this would exponentially increase the likelihood of the businesses being found at fault for a data breach despite having overall reasonable data security standards, because the FTC would potentially only need to find unreasonableness as to any one of the factors in order to claim a violation of the Act.

As the FTC has found previously, a multi-factor test is appropriate under GLBA guidelines for more sophisticated entities such as financial institutions because they routinely have much broader sets of the most sensitive personal and financial customer information in digitized form, which presents security risks and vulnerabilities not evident in most unregulated commercial businesses with much narrower data sets that typically contain less sensitive customer information. Additionally, financial institutions are subject to an examination process in which they work with bank examiners to develop a security plan that is in compliance with their guidance.

As discussed in detail in my written testimony, the FTC does not have staff or processes capable of providing this guidance process to every business under its jurisdiction, and entities subject to its jurisdiction may only become aware of the possibility of being in non-compliance with an FTC-enforced standard when they are under investigation. Under its broad jurisdiction, FTC enforcement of a multi-factor test would apply to every non-financial institution in the country, including not only retailers, but hotels, bars and restaurants, theaters, auto dealers, gas stations, grocery and convenience stores, fast-food eateries, airlines and others in the travel industry, hospitals and doctors, dentists, veterinarians, hair salons, gyms, dry cleaners, plumbers and taxi drivers. These businesses do not have the staff to determine up-front whether they could survive a mult-factor test. Virtually every unregulated business in the U.S. economy that provides goods or services to American consumers. Imposing Banking regulatory standards on these unregulated businesses, to be enforced by the FTC in a non-examination process, would be an unprecedented expansion of FTC authority comparable to what the commission attempted to accomplish with its "red flags" rule, before congress was forced to intervene.

Question 2. Do you think the 51 different breach notification laws create confusion for consumers—especially for those who move, travel frequently, or live in an area where they shop and work across state lines?

Answer. Yes. We have reached the point where these laws not only require different notification standards, but many suffer from a flawed rule that leads to overnotification. Specifically, the third-party entity rules in state breach laws do not require those entities to provide notification to affected consumers when they are breached. As further explained in my written testimony, to have an effective breach law, these "notice holes" must be closed. This is a position that the retail industry has successfully conveyed to, and favorably recognized, by certain State AGs. For example, a payment processor who works with multiple merchants could, under many state laws, fulfill its obligations by requiring dozens of merchants to bear the burden of providing varying notices to the same consumers for the processor's single breach. Such a rule does not provide effective notice to consumers; rather, it results in likely over-notification and confusion as consumers receive multiple and differing notices about the same breach from entities that did not suffer the breach.

The most effective and timely consumer notice would result from a nationwide standard that requires all breached entities—including all breached third-party entities—to provide public notice, either directly to the affected consumers or via a substitute notification procedure where they make the breach publicly known through widely distributed media and other acceptable means. Some flexibility should be provided to respect contractual arrangements between third-party contractors and those that hire them regarding the most effective notice, but the general rule should clearly place the burden for requiring notice and any potential liability for the breach on the breached entity.

This threat of making public disclosure has proven to be a powerful incentive to companies to improve their data security standards. A Federal bill that preempts state laws has the opportunity to close the problematic notice holes that exist in state laws for third-party entities and provide not only more robust notification—leading to greater consumer protection and awareness of data breaches that may cause financial harm—but also create "skin in the game" for all entities so that they place greater emphasis on, and investment in, improving data security for the most sensitive data.

———

RESPONSE TO WRITTEN QUESTIONS SUBMITTED BY HON. JERRY MORAN TO DOUG JOHNSON

Question 1. During the hearing, a statement was made saying that "three times more data breaches occur at financial institutions than at retailers" citing a report by Verizon. Will you please share your analysis of this data provided in the referenced Verizon report?

Answer. The Identity Theft Resource Center has compiled a list of all publicly reported breaches in the United States and shows that banks accounted for only 5.5 percent of all breaches in 2014. Other businesses accounted for 33 percent. Retailer groups continue to cite the Verizon report on data breach statistics as a way to distract policymakers regarding the primary focus of data security breaches, but the inconvenient truth is that this Verizon report is based on an international sample of breaches as opposed to an actual compilation of all publicly reported breaches in the United States.

Question 2. In some of the testimony, it was stated that one cause of the major breaches at Target and Home Depot, and perhaps similar breaches, was an "easily forged signature." From your perspective, what other causes have you identified as contributors to these breaches?

Answer. Forged signatures were not a cause in the Target, Home Depot, or any similar breach. The major cause of these breaches were the insecure point of sale systems used by these retailers. Bank customer credit and debit card numbers would not have been breached if these systems had not been vulnerable to POS malware. The card numbers also would not have been breached if Target had properly segregated its POS system from an invoicing system that Fazio Mechanical Services, a vendor to Target, had access to. When Fazio Mechanical was compromised with malicious software it gave the criminals a direct tunnel to Target's POS system, which allowed the criminals to install additional malicious software on that system.

Question 3. As lawmakers consider a national data breach notification standard, it has been suggested that some industries should have an exception because they are governed by other breach laws. What are the pros and cons of creating an exemption for financial institutions? Is it possible that a Gramm-Leach-Bliley Act exemption would create "notice holes" where consumers would not receive notices of breaches at banks and other financial institutions?

Answer. A Gramm-Leach-Bliley Act (GLBA) exemption from a national breach notification standard, rather than creating a "notice hole," is appropriate in that we recommend any national standard imposed on other industries should be consistent with GLBA.

As we enact a national data breach requirement, some industries—including the financial industry—are already required by law to develop and maintain robust internal protections to combat and address criminal attacks, and are required to protect consumer financial information and notify consumers when a breach occurs within their systems that will put their customers at risk.

Title V of GLBA requires banks to implement a "risk-based" response program to address instances of unauthorized access to customer information systems. At a minimum, a response program must:

1. Assess the nature and scope of any security incident and identify what customer information systems and customer information may have been accessed or misused;

2. Notify the institution's primary Federal regulator "as soon as possible" about any threats "to sensitive customer information."

3. Notify appropriate law enforcement authorities and file Suspicious Activity Reports in situations involving Federal criminal violations requiring immediate attention;

4. Take appropriate steps to contain the incident to prevent further unauthorized access to or use of customer information, and

5. Notify customers "as soon as possible" if it is determined that misuse of customer information has occurred or is reasonably possible.

A critical component of the GLBA guidelines is customer notification. When a covered financial institution becomes aware of a material breach of "sensitive customer information," it must conduct a reasonable investigation to determine whether the information has been or can be misused. If it determines that misuse of the information "has occurred or is reasonably possible," it must notify affected customers "as soon as possible."

Under GLBA, sensitive customer information includes the customer's name, address or telephone number in conjunction with the customer's Social Security number, driver's license number, credit card, debit card or other account number or personal identification number. Sensitive customer information also includes any combination of components of customer information that would allow someone to log onto or access the customer's account, such as user name and password.

A covered financial institution must also provide a clear and conspicuous notice. The notice must describe the incident in general terms and the type of customer information affected. It must also generally describe the institution's actions to protect the information from further unauthorized access and include a telephone number. The notice also must remind customers to remain vigilant over the next 12 to 24 months and to promptly report incidents of suspected identity theft to the institution.

Where appropriate, the notice also must include:

1. Recommendation to review account statements immediately and report suspicious activity;

2. Description of fraud alerts and how to place them;

3. Recommendation that the customer periodically obtain credit reports and have fraudulent information removed;

4. Explanation of how to receive a free credit report; and

5. Information about the FTC's identity theft guidance for consumers.

In summary, rather than creating a notice hole, we believe the extensive breach reporting requirements currently in place for banks provide an effective basis for any national data breach reporting requirement for businesses generally.

Question 4. Do you think requiring the use of PINs on payment transactions is the best solution for addressing the data breach problem? What aspects of the increased use of PIN technology would be helpful in preventing future data breaches? In your estimation, are there drawbacks to increasing PIN use? Please share any additional insight on the use of PIN technology that you feel may be useful to the Committee as it explores data breach prevention. Also, please comment on new and emerging payment technologies and potential security advantages or vulnerabilities.

Answer. The fact is that attackers are becoming increasingly adept at defeating cybersecurity practices and mitigating measures points to the need for industry to develop and deploy enhanced measures on an ongoing basis with greater speed. Rather than adopting static number PIN technology, we intend to focus on taking static numbers out of the payment system entirely.

Eliminating the use of static numbers altogether for debit and credit card purchases is a very important next step in protecting our payment system and the consumers that use it. Finding ways to keep consumers from having to remember static numbers, letters or symbols in order to authenticate themselves when conducting a financial or other sensitive transaction was a primary focus at the recent White House Summit on Cybersecurity and Consumer Protection. For instance:

- *Ajay Banga, President and CEO, MasterCard:* ''What I have learned from my consumer customers is that they want two clear things aside from safety and security—one is to stop making me remember things to prove I am who I am. Because there are too many things to remember.''
- *Richard Davis, Chairman and CEO, U.S. Bank:* ''Our job is really a lot of financial literacy to help people understand how to protect themselves better . . . not putting a piece of tape on the back of your debit card or credit card and writing your PIN on it.''
- *Chuck Scharf, CEO, Visa:* We can talk all we want about methods of authentication . . . but the fact is if card numbers are flying around even though there is zero liability it's not something the consumer wants to go through . . . We are working with people across the payment ecosystem to figure out where we can get rid of those account numbers, so if there is a compromise, which there always will be because the bad guys are steps ahead as hard as we all try, the compromise does not have the effect it has today.''

These comments point to the fact that payment security is a dynamic challenge that requires a like response, and that there is no single solution that will eliminate payment fraud. Locking in any static technology provides a roadmap to attackers, telling them where to focus their attacks. Tokenization replaces sensitive consumer account information at the register or online with a random ''token,'' rendering any static information associated with the transaction useless to criminals, and thus shows great promise.

RESPONSE TO WRITTEN QUESTIONS SUBMITTED BY HON. ROY BLUNT TO DOUG JOHNSON

Question 1. Today, there are 51 different laws dealing with breach notification, and another 12 dealing with security requirements—with even more states considering new laws, or changing their existing laws.

Given this trend, do you think Federal data breach legislation should include a clear national standard for both data security and breach notification?

Answer. Although some of these laws are similar, many have inconsistent and conflicting standards, forcing businesses to comply with multiple regulations and leaving many consumers without proper recourse and protections. Inconsistent state laws and regulations should be preempted in favor of strong Federal data protection and notification requirements. In the event of a breach, the public should be informed where it occurred as soon as reasonably possible to allow consumers to protect themselves from fraud.

We believe that the following set of principles should serve as a guide when drafting legislation to provide stronger protection for consumer financial information:

1. Inconsistent state laws and regulations should be preempted in favor of strong Federal data protection and notification standards.
2. Strong national data protection and consumer notification standards with effective enforcement provisions must be part of any comprehensive data security regime, applicable to any party with access to important consumer financial information.
3. Requirements for industries that are already subject to robust data protection and notification requirements must be recognized.
4. In the event of a breach, the public should be informed where it occurred as soon as reasonably possible to allow consumers to protect themselves from fraud. The business with the most direct financial relationship with affected consumers should be able to inform their customers and members about information regarding the breach, including the entity at which the breach occurred.
5. The costs of a data breach should ultimately be borne by the entity that incurs the breach.

Our existing national payments system serves hundreds of millions of consumers, retailers, banks, and the economy well. It only stands to reason that such a system functions most effectively when it is governed by a consistent national data breach policy.

Question 2. Do you feel the standards and guidance under Gramm-Leach-Bliley provide necessary security, but with flexibility for organizations of different size and complexity? If so, can you elaborate why?

Answer. Effective data protection requirements are scalable. For instance, bank regulations, through GLBA, recognize that the level of risk to customer data varies significantly across banks. Large banks require continual, on-site examination personnel, while community-based institutions are subject to periodic information security examinations.

Data security is also an ongoing process as opposed to the state or condition of controls at a point in time.

As opposed to proscribing specific technological security requirements, GLBA and the associated bank regulatory requirements are risk and governance-based. Bank security programs are required to have "strong board and senior management level support, integration of security activities and controls throughout the organization's business processes, and clear accountability for carrying out security responsibilities."

Question 3. Hackers seem to be getting more sophisticated by the day, and I imagine we expect even more attacks and perhaps more successful ones in the future. If that is the case doesn't it make sense to do everything possible to protect consumer personal and financial data? Do you think Federal data security standards applicable to all players in the payments process would help and if so why?

Answer. Any legislation focused on creating a national standard for breach notification should also include a complementary national data security standard for covered entities. If Congress does not address data security standards now it misses the opportunity to instill a greater overall level of data security protections for consumers.

Because the payment system is by definition a network, *every* business within that network must share in the responsibility to protect consumers and should have to abide by a data security standard. With that responsibility should also come the requirement for that business, whether it be a bank, merchant, third party processor or other entity, to bear the costs for any breach they incur.

Question 4. A number of states have enacted data protection and consumer notification laws. However, I also understand that these provisions can vary from state to state. Is your industry currently covered by any Federal law that requires consumer financial and personal data to be protected? Are there other industries that are not covered by Federal data protection and consumer notification standards?

Answer. Yes, Title V of GLBA requires banks to implement a "risk-based" response program to address instances of unauthorized access to customer information systems. At a minimum, a response program must:

1. Assess the nature and scope of any security incident and identify what customer information systems and customer information may have been accessed or misused;

2. Notify the institution's primary Federal regulator "as soon as possible" about any threats "to sensitive customer information."

3. Notify appropriate law enforcement authorities and file Suspicious Activity Reports in situations involving Federal criminal violations requiring immediate attention;

4. Take appropriate steps to contain the incident to prevent further unauthorized access to or use of customer information, and

5. Notify customers "as soon as possible" if it is determined that misuse of customer information has occurred or is reasonably possible.

As already noted, the GLBA also contains a set of scalable data security standards. The retail industry currently does not currently have a similar set of Federal requirements. The legal, regulatory, examination and enforcement regime regarding banks ensures that banks robustly protect American's personal financial information. We believe that this regime provides an appropriate, scalable model for other businesses entrusted with sensitive customer financial and other information.

RESPONSE TO WRITTEN QUESTIONS SUBMITTED BY HON. ROY BLUNT TO YAEL WEINMAN

Question 1. Today, there are 51 different laws dealing with breach notification, and another 12 dealing with security requirements—with even more states considering new laws, or changing their existing laws.

Given this trend, do you think Federal data breach legislation should include a clear national standard for both data security and breach notification?

Answer. ITI supports a breach notification bill that preempts state notification requirements consistent with our breach notification principles (previously submitted for the record and attached hereto). It is critically necessary to replace the existing 51 state and territory notification laws with one national framework. While ITI does not seek a national data security requirement in such a bill, we would not oppose a bill that includes a reasonable and technology-neutral data security requirement that is appropriate to a company's size and complexity, the nature and scope of its activities, and the sensitivity of the data held, and that preempts existing and future state data security requirements.

Question 2. Do you think the 51 different breach notification laws create confusion for consumers—especially for those who move, travel frequently, or live in an area where they shop and work across state lines?

Answer. Consistency in notices would reduce consumer confusion that may result from the variances of the method of data breach notifications, the content of such notifications, and the circumstances of such notification. In addition, consistency would also reduce confusion for businesses—particularly smaller e-commerce businesses—as to how and when to notify their customers who reside in different states, each requiring a different type or content for notification and under differing circumstances.

Æ

73

This page intentionally left blank.

74

This page intentionally left blank.

75

This page intentionally left blank.